SELLING THE HUMANITIES

ESSAYS

JEFFREY R. DI LEO

If the humanities are to make a difference in public life, does that mean we have to say that they are instrumental to some other social good?

—Judith Butler, "Ordinary, Incredulous" (2014)

Library of Congress Cataloging-in-Publication Data

Names: Di Leo, Jeffrey R., author. | Veeser, H. Aram (Harold Aram),
   1950-writer of afterword.
Title: Selling the humanities : essays / Jeffrey R. Di Leo ; with an
   afterword by H. Aram Veeser.
Description: First edition. | Huntsville, Texas : TRP: The University
   Press of SHSU, [2023] | Includes bibliographical references.
Identifiers: LCCN 2023014178 (print) | LCCN 2023014179 (ebook) |
   ISBN 9781680033182 (paperback) | ISBN 9781680033199 (ebook)
Subjects: LCSH: Humanities--Philosophy. | Humanities--Study and
   teaching (Higher) | Humanities--Economic aspects. | Humanities-
   -History--21st century. | LCGFT: Essays.
Classification: LCC AZ103 .D55 2023 (print) | LCC AZ103 (ebook) |
   DDC 001.301--dc23/eng/20230413
LC record available at https://lccn.loc.gov/2023014178
LC ebook record available at https://lccn.loc.gov/2023014179

FIRST EDITION

Front cover image courtesy: Shutterstock

Cover design by Bradley Alan Ivey
Interior design by Bradley Alan Ivey

TRP: The University Press of SHSU
Huntsville, Texas 77341
texasreviewpress.org

CONTENTS

PREFACE

You might think of it as a "fire" sale.

Some items, such as the Great Books, have been under fire since the culture wars of the 1990s. Others, such as theory, sustained extensive smoke damage at the hands of cultural studies and conservative critics shortly thereafter. And still more, such as *critique*, have only recently been charred by postcritics desperately trying to put out the smoldering flames of the humanities.

Now, however, the fires have been extinguished and the humanities are for sale. Slightly worse from smoke and fire damage, but still salvageable. Those who have dedicated their lives to the humanities live in precarious times that call for some crucial decision-making. This book discusses some of the decisions they face and argues that the humanities fire sale must be taken seriously.

It also argues that the worst part of it all may not be the damage itself done by the fires in the humanities. But rather that much of it was self-inflicted.

Just before the financial bubble burst in 2008, there was arrogance in the air about the need to defend the humanities against its critics. While it was acceptable for humanities scholars to work out their doctrinal differences among themselves—and in the process, effectively burn down each other's doctrinal house—those outside of the humanities pack needed to stay out of these internal fights. At the time, one of the leaders of the pack was the literary critic Stanley Fish. It was hard not to hear his voice because it seemed to be everywhere about everything concerning the humanities and the university. High profile venues such as the *Chronicle of Higher Education*, *Harper's*, *The New York Times*, and *New York Times Book Review* ran his opinion pieces in continuous play.

From Fish's perspective, the major culprits of the crisis in the humanities were the professors who mixed politics with pedagogy, and the state and federal legislators "who are supposedly in charge of ensuring the health and prosperity of higher education." The former, in Fish's opinion, needed to refocus their energies on their teaching and research, not social and political advocacy. The latter—who Fish notoriously dealt with directly for a brief time as a dean—needed to keep their noses out of our classrooms, and leave the university and its operation to the academics.

By his own admission, Fish dealt rather harshly with politicians who weighed in on university matters. "In the course of several years," he writes in *Save the World on Your Own Time* (2008), "I said many nasty things about members of Congress, Illinois state representatives and senators, the governor of Illinois, the governor's budget director, and the governor-appointed Illinois Board of Higher Education." "I called these people ignorant, misinformed, demagogic, and dishonest and repeatedly suggested that when it came to colleges and universities, either they didn't know what they were talking about or (and this is worse) they did know and were deliberately setting out to destroy public education."

Moreover, when it came to defending the value of the humanities against its critics at the state and federal level, Fish recommended that we shouldn't we even try. "Instead of defending the classics or French literature or sociology," said Fish, "ask those who think they need defending what they know about them, and if the answer is 'not much' (on the model of 'don't know much about the Middle Ages'), suggest, ever so politely, that they might want to go back to school." "Instead of trying to justify your values (always a weak position), assume them and assume too your right to define and protect them," continues Fish. "And when you are invited to explain, defend, or justify, just say no."

The problem with this position is that after the economic collapse of 2008, there was no longer the *option* to not explain, defend, or justify the value of the humanities. The rise of the neoliberal university wherein every aspect of its operation is assessed and managed through a financial lens, not an academic one, accelerated after the economic bubble burst. In the aftermath, the humanities increasingly became just one more dimension of a fully managed business aimed at vocational training. While it might be heterodox and antagonistic to say, as Fish does, that universities and colleges "are not businesses," when those who pay bills do not agree with this position, it signals bad times ahead for the humanities. If anyone in this scenario needed to go "back to school," it was academics who did not know the principles of management and marketing which are required knowledge to successfully run academic institutions in the age of extreme market fundamentalism.

Of course, Fish was not the only one making the argument that universities are not businesses, but he was probably the loudest and most vocal proponent of this position. The problem with this line of argument is that it did nothing to prepare the humanities for the critique of its value and consequent defunding that occurred in the aftermath of the economic collapse of 2008. The rise of the fully managed neoliberal university brought with it the requirement that every area within its purview demonstrate its value relative to the goal of training students for the workforce. The humanities no longer had the luxury to fashion itself as transcending the world of economic and business values. It came to be required, at least within the academic setting, that the humanities *demonstrate* its economic value in a way that the people Fish called "ignorant, misinformed, demagogic, and dishonest" could understand. But how does one do this? How does one sell the humanities to a neoliberal value system where the market is the sole-determinant of value?

One way to look at the life of the humanities after the economic collapse of 2008 is to view it as a series of efforts to find a successful way of selling the humanities in the age of late capitalism. The recent pandemic has only amplified this situation with most institutions dedicated to supporting the humanities struggling to stay financially above water. If the effect of the economic crisis of 2008 over the course of the next dozen years was to turn the humanities into a business operation, then one might wager that the effect of the pandemic of 2020 will be to turn advocates of the humanities into full-blown salesmen—or, if you will, salespeople.

Arthur Miller famously couldn't decide whether *Death of a Salesman* was "the tragedy of a man who gave his life, or sold it" in pursuit of the American Dream. For the emerging generation of humanities salespeople, a similar dilemma holds. In working to sell the humanities to colleges and universities, to the benefactors who support them, to the agencies which fund them, to the public which benefits from them, and to all of the other institutions which support them including the world of publishing, we face a truly existential crisis: are we giving our lives to the humanities or selling them in their pursuit?

3

It may be an open question whether the drama we are now living is about those who gave their life in pursuit of the humanities or those who have sold it. But it is not open to debate that we are all participants in a living *tragedy* regarding the humanities. Also, it is not open to debate that we need to work together to find better ways to sell the humanities to those who cannot find any value in them.

Academics like Fish who only aim to antagonize in order to draw attention to themselves work against a future for the humanities. A decade or two ago this type of behavior may have been prime viewing on academic Showtime, but today those who exhibit it may themselves need to go "back to school." The fate of the humanities is in the hands of those who can balance arguments regarding the value of the humanities with a critique of the neoliberalism in all of its forms. To do so is to walk the proverbial "razor's edge" as a committed, progressive humanities advocate.

Selling the Humanities explores the challenges facing literature, philosophy, and theory at a time when the humanities appear to some as burnt out. There is incredible pressure to demonstrate the value of the humanities within institutions dedicated to economic feasibility and job placement, not intellectual power and social commitment. This situation is further intensified by the demand that one must always be prepared to sell the humanities to others in an effort to save them. But is it even possible to commodify the humanities? And if so, might our efforts to sell the humanities also have the potential to kill them in the process?

The essays here take up these and other topics regarding the situation of the humanities today by glancing backward to the thoughts of some of its forgotten heroes for inspiration and strength, and looking forward through the eyes of scholars who are working toward a future for the humanities. My own perspective is that of a philosopher who served for a decade and a half as a university dean and has edited a humanities journal for twice that amount of time. From this vantage point, selling the humanities in order to save them is a task that should not just be left to a handful of high-profile public intellectuals—but one required of anyone and everyone who cares about the future of the humanities. Selling the humanities is the business of everyone who values them.

1 | HAPPINESS FOR SALE

"It is not difficult to be unhappy or discontented," wrote the philosopher Émile Chartier.

"All you have to do is sit down, like a prince waiting to be amused," he continues. "This attitude of lying in wait and weighing happiness as if it were a commodity casts the gray shadow of boredom over everything."

Chartier was a French philosopher who died in 1951 at the age of 83. He spent his entire professional career teaching philosophy in secondary schools. Though his star has dimmed over the years, while he was alive, he was considered by the French as the most important philosopher since René Descartes. His pupils included Raymond Aron, Simone de Beauvoir, Georges Canguilhem, André Maurois, Maurice Schuman, and Simone Weil. He has also been called the greatest teacher of their generation.

"The key to [Chartier's] teaching," writes John Hellman in *Simone Weil* (1982), "was his determination to instill critical habits of mind in his students." "He believed," continues Hellman, "that students did not truly 'acquire' ideas until they had digested them and re-expressed them in their own words." Rather than in-class exams, he thus preferred to assign "'topos,' or take-home essay examinations, to his students which forced them to formulate their own (not 'correct') answers to knotty questions."

To be sure, Chartier's pedagogical prowess was as legendary as some of his pupils. Still, the work of his closest contemporary, Henri Bergson, is much more highly regarded today than that of Chartier. Part of the reason is the ephemeral nature of the majority of his writing. That is, while he published numerous books on philosophical topics, he was best known in France through the thousands of articles he published in various daily newspapers. Beginning in 1903, he started to publish these philosophical articles under the pseudonym "Alain," a name he took from the fifteenth-century Norman poet, Alain Chartier.

At first Alain's articles were longer weekly columns and then in 1906 they became daily short articles. The shorter articles were published as a daily column entitled *Propos d'un Normand*. From 1906 until the start of the Great War in 1914, Alain wrote a two page article every evening. Then, after the war—which he fought in as a soldier even though he was exempt from service and could have served as an officer—he resumed the practice of writing *propos*. All said and done, Alain produced nearly 5,000 of these little articles.

Turning philosophy into literature or journalism can be difficult for philosophers. Writing for a philosophical audience is very different than writing for a literary or general one. Certain assumptions that are made when writing for a philosophical audience cannot be made for a general audience. As such, the list of philosophers of note who successfully wrote for a general audience is a short one.

Alain was able to bridge this gap through the technique he used to write his little articles. Every evening he would sit down with two sheets of paper in front of him. He then started to write his *propos* knowing that its last line would be at the bottom of the second page. He also committed himself to making no corrections, erasures, or changes. This allowed him to meet his publication deadline (all pieces were published the next day) and write only that which was directly relevant to the topic of the *propos*. The result was thousands of 50 to 60 line aphoristic compositions.

In 1928, ninety-three of Alain's *propos* dealing with the theme of happiness (*bonheur*) were published as *Propos sur le bonheur*, which became a best-selling book. The lines above are from the penultimate *propos* in this collection entitled "The Obligation to be Happy." It is dated March 16, 1923, and was entitled as to leave no doubt as to his position on happiness. It was a position steeped in practical wisdom tempered with an endless bounty of cheerfulness and cheeky irony. Alain encouraged people to not complain or burden others with their problems. Rather, even when the chips are down, he encouraged his readers to present a happy face. For Alain, those who *choose* to be happy will be the recipients of great rewards.

As someone who experienced first-hand the horrors of the Great War and regarded war itself to be an absolute evil, Alain believed observance of his practical wisdom about happiness might have resulted in avoiding this epic catastrophe. "For it is my opinion that all these cadavers, all these ruins and wild expenditures and precautionary offensives," wrote Alain, are the work of men who have never managed to be happy and who cannot abide those who *try to be.*" The last words here are emphasized to point out that happiness is something that we need to continuously work at by vowing to ourselves that we will be happy and by teaching happiness to others including our students and children.

Alain's aphoristic approach to happiness is perfect for a world that needs help in recovering from a great catastrophe. There is no grand philosophical position on happiness other than practical wisdom such as monitoring your moods and getting plenty of exercise. Eventually, this type of happiness or well-being journalism became commonplace in newspapers through regular features on relationship advice (e.g., "Dear Abby"), health and beauty tips, self-remedies, and recreational guides.

My favorite though in this mix is the daily horoscope, which is the ultimate happiness tool: "The stars show the kind of day you'll have!"

Thus, the most visible remainder of Alain's philosophical contribution is the happiness journalism that is still a feature of many daily newspapers.

ક•

Alain's optimism about happiness though is not the typical twentieth-century position.

The Great War set the tone for a much more pessimistic approach. Arguably, the *rejection* of happiness and its pursuit is one of the cornerstones of the modern condition and modernity.

A good place to see this typically modern position on happiness is found in the writings of Sigmund Freud, particularly his *Civilization and Its Discontents*, which was published in 1929, a year after the release of Alain's *Propos sur le bonheur.*

Very early in his career, while working with Josef Breuer on their jointly published *Studies on Hysteria* (1895), Freud writes of a common objection to his treatment by patients:

7

> "Why, you tell me yourself that my illness is probably connected with my circumstances and the events of my life. You cannot alter these in any way. How do you propose to help me, then?"

To which Freud replies:

> "No doubt fate would find it easier than I do to relieve you of your illness. But you will be able to convince yourself that much will be gained if we succeed in transforming your hysterical misery into uncommon unhappiness. With a mental life that has been restored to health you will be better armed against that unhappiness."

But it is really with the introduction of the "destructive instinct" or the death drive that Freud places something other than happiness as the goal of life.

In *Beyond the Pleasure Principle*, which was first published in 1920, twenty-five years after his work with Breuer, Freud introduces the death instinct. "If we are to take it as a truth that knows no exception that everything living dies for *internal* reasons—becomes inorganic once again—then we shall be compelled to say that 'the goal of all life is death,'" writes Freud, "and, looking backwards, that 'what was inanimate existed before what is living.'"

He would later formally link the "life instinct" (Eros) to the "death instinct" (Thanatos). Together, they are the only basic instincts. "The aim of the first of these basic instincts is to establish even greater unities and to preserve them thus—in short, to bind together; the aim of the second, on the contrary, is to undo connections and so to destroy things." For Freud, "the final aim of the destructive instinct is to reduce living things to an inorganic state."

Along with these two primal forces is the "pleasure principle," which Freud describes as "a tendency operating in the service of a function whose business it is to free the mental apparatus from excitation or to keep the amount of excitation in it constant or to keep it as low as possible." As to whether the pleasure principle "requires a reduction, or perhaps ultimately the extinction, of the tension of the instinctual needs (that is, a state of *Nirvana*) leads to problems that are still unexamined in the relations between the pleasure principle and the two primal forces, Eros and the death instinct." So, while we have the unexamined potential for Nirvana in Freud, what about happiness?

In *Civilization and Its Discontents*, Freud leaves no doubt as to his position on happiness. While it can hardly be doubted that people "seek happiness, they want to become happy and to remain so," this conflicts with both our basic instincts and the world. According to Freud,

> the pleasure-principle draws up the programme [sic] of life's purpose. This principle dominates the operation of the mental apparatus from the very beginning; there can be no doubt about its efficiency, and yet its programme [sic] is in conflict with the whole world, with the macrocosm as much as with the microcosm. It simply cannot be put into execution, the whole constitution of things runs counter to it; one might say the intention that man should be "happy" is not included in the scheme of "Creation." What is called happiness in its narrowest sense comes from the satisfaction—most often instantaneous—of pent-up needs which have reached great intensity, and by its very nature can only be a transitory experience. When any condition desired by the pleasure-principle is protracted, it results in a feeling only of mild comfort; we are so constituted that we can only intensely enjoy contrasts, much less intensely states themselves. Our possibilities of happiness are thus limited from the start by our very constitution. It is much less difficult to be unhappy.

For Freud, not only does the present state of civilization "inadequately provid[e] us with what we require to make us happy in life," so too does "the scheme of 'Creation.'" Thus, while unhappiness *is* readily attainable, happiness *is not*. To expect otherwise goes against the fundamental tenets of psychoanalysis.

In psychoanalysis, Jacques Lacan would continue to develop in novel ways the critique of happiness that Freud initiated. For Lacan, "Freud leaves no doubt, any more than Aristotle, that what man is seeking, his goal, is happiness." However, referring to the passage above by Freud about the conflict between happiness and the world, writes Lacan, "I prefer to read in *Civilization and Its Discontents* the idea Freud expresses there concerning happiness, namely, that absolutely nothing is prepared for it, either in macrocosm or microcosm."

9

Today, Slavoj Žižek, perhaps the most popular philosopher in the world, continues to champion the psychoanalytic critique of happiness developed by Freud and Lacan. And though he approaches it from many different directions and contexts, the core tenets of Žižek's approach remain consistent: psychoanalysis establishes happiness as "the betrayal of desire." For Žižek, happiness is "not a category of truth, but a category of mere Being, and, as such, confused, indeterminate, inconsistent"—a position most definitely contra that of the happiness journalism of Alain.

৯

"Clap along," sings Pharrell Williams, "if you feel like happiness is the truth."

And people in the United States and around the world did—in record numbers.

Released in June of 2013, Pharrell's "Happy" was the best-selling song in the U.S. in 2014 with 6.45 million copies sold. In the United Kingdom, it sold more than 1.6 million copies in 2014 making it the most downloaded track *ever* in the UK beating out Robin Thicke's "Blurred Lines" and Adele's "Someone Like You," which respectively sold 1.59 and 1.53 million copies each. In the first quarter of 2014 "Happy" was streamed a mind-boggling 43 million times on Pandora. Still, these streams only resulted in $2,700 in publisher and songwriter royalties, which did not make Pharrell too happy and led him to join a group of artists demanding that YouTube take down thousands of songs it did not have permission to use. In the case of "Happy," the song was used frequently on YouTube as background music to international expressions of "happiness."

Literally thousands of videos can be found on YouTube of people from around the world dancing to Pharrell's hit song. In fact, by May of 2014, there were more than 1,500 videos including an independently launched website (wearehappyfrom.com) to showcase them. For example, there is a video of folks in the High Tatras Mountains in Slovakia swinging to his song against breathtaking landscape that has been viewed 7.3 million times since it was posted in March of 2014. There is also a video from Australia of shots of "happy" dogs and cats posted in May of 2014 that had 14.3 million views, double that of the High Tatras video, perhaps implying that the happiness of our animal friends is just as "true" worldwide as that of their human keepers. Then, of course, there is the YouTube video of the Minions dancing to Pharrell's international hit. Posted in June of 2013, the Minions "Happy" video has been viewed 76.7 million times. Still, the viewership of these "Happy" videos pales next to the number of views of the Official Music Video of "Happy" by Pharrell Williams. Posted on November 21, 2013, it has now been viewed over *one billion times*—1,081,323,789 times to be exact.

To say that this song has been wildly popular worldwide is substantiated by both its sales figures and the many videos done by people wanting to share with others expressions of their happiness. But this song is just a small piece of a much larger industry centered on the development, promotion, and sale of "happiness" as a product. It is an industry connected to among other things a new branch of psychology, the rise of big data, and the military industrial complex. The exponential rise and growth of the happiness industry both is fueled by and fuels the blissful belief so directly put in Pharrell's song that "happiness is the truth."

In just the few examples from YouTube noted above, all are used to sell products: the Slovaks want us to vacation in the High Tatras Mountains so use a thumbnail view of a woman in a bikini to get viewers to successfully click what is essentially a tourism video; the Australian video, while foregoing bikinis, uses an even more effective clickbait tool, the dog and cat video, to lure viewers into what is essentially a promotional video for an "off leash training program" for dogs which offers a "doggy outing service," wherein up to a dozen dogs are picked up by the dog trainer and taken to a dog friendly place to play and practice their training, and are then taken home after getting a rinse and a nail trim, if needed; the Minions video of "Happy" was used to promote the film, *Despicable Me 2*, for which the song was originally written before it eventually landed on Pharrell's 2014 album G I R L. Apparently though it took him a long time to reach an agreement with the film studio about the song.

"My song submissions for this scene [in *Despicable Me 2*] were rejected nine times," says Pharrell in a New York Times op-ed. Of this long process to produce a hit song for a 76 million dollar film that grossed 970 million dollars worldwide, one critic writes, "Looks like we could have lived in a world where 'Happy' did not exist"—or at least was not as profitable.

11

But in spite of the overwhelming international response to Pharrell's song, which at less than four minutes in length manages to sing the word "happy" almost sixty times, some people—not named Freud—were not so happy with "Happy." A YouTube video from May of 2014 set to "Happy" by some Iranian fans led to their arrest. The police chief said the song represented public vulgarity and also hurt public chastity. The president of Iran, Hassan Rouhani criticized the arrest in a May 21, 2014 tweet saying "#Happiness is our people's right. We shouldn't be too hard on behaviors caused by joy." Though the director and the dancers were later released, they each received a suspended punishment of 91 lashes. This means that if within a period of three years they commit *another* crime then their lashing will be carried out.

Chartier said that happiness is not a commodity—but it sure sold a lot of newspapers in France.

And based on the response to Pharrell's song, it is still selling well a century later.

Pharrell's "Happy" peaked at Number 1 in the music charts of nineteen countries.

Moreover, even arguments *against happiness* sell well. Žižek is an international favorite, whose two-minute YouTube lecture against happiness has been viewed 1.6 million times.

Madison Avenue built an industry on selling happiness. Psychology in America was co-opted in the early twentieth century by business interests eager for findings that could be used to better determine and control consumer behavior. Key to this co-optation was the behavioral psychology of John B. Watson, which soon became the property of the Madison Avenue advertising industry.

In 1920, Watson joined J. Walter Thompson, a large Madison Avenue advertising firm, at four times the salary that he was earning at Johns Hopkins University. By this time, the advertising industry—excited by the potential of using psychology to increase its effectiveness—was willing to pay intellectuals to work on behalf of business. Even Theodor Adorno was pulled into this orbit by working on a study for CBS of its radio audiences.

Also, in addition to the birth of advertising science based on the psychology of happiness, there was a growing demand among managers and policy makers for a science of workplace happiness, which included the development of better elevator music. Today, however, American psychiatry is completely cut out of the happiness industry to the point where 80% of the prescriptions for antidepressant drugs in the U.S. are written not by psychiatrists, but rather by medical doctors and primary care practitioners. Moreover, the use of antidepressant drugs such as Prozac has reached epidemic proportions.

To be sure, happiness today is a commodity—and it may very well be the best-selling product on Amazon. The free market rewards consumer demand with more products. The axioms of neoliberalism dictate that *everything* is for sale and that everything can—and should be—plundered for profit including happiness.

What Freud and Lacan say about happiness is only background noise when we are dancing "happily" with the Minions.

But maybe Alain still has something to teach us about happiness—and maybe it is not found in the story of Pharrell's corporate music experience but comes from one of the greatest bands in the world—the Rolling Stones.

Compare Pharrel's experience of writing "Happy" to Keith Richards writing a song of the same title for the Rolling Stones album *Exile on Main Street* (1972).

"We did ["Happy"] in an afternoon," writes Richards in his autobiography, *Life* (2010).

> [I]n only four hours, cut and done. At four o'clock it was on tape. It was no Rolling Stones record. It's got the name on it, but it was actually Jimmy Miller on drums, Bobby Keys on baritone and that was basically it. And then I overdubbed bass and guitar. We were just waiting for everybody to turn up for the real sessions for the rest of the night and we thought, we're here; let's see if we can come up with something. I'd written it that day.

The words to the song "just came tripping off the tongue," says Richards.

"I need a love to keep me happy. I need a love to keep me happy."

While a hit for the Rolling Stones, it was written much like Alain's *propos*.

If happiness *is* for sale, then I'm buying the one that Keith Richards exiled on Main Street.

13

2 | THE WRITER'S JOURNAL

"I've never kept a journal—or rather I've never known if I should keep one. Sometimes I begin, and then, right away, I leave off—and yet, later on, I begin again. The impulse is faint, intermittent, without seriousness and of no doctrinal standing whatever. I guess I could diagnose this *diary disease:* insoluble doubt as to the value of what one writes in it."

—Roland Barthes, "Deliberation" (1979)

A fourteen-year-old teenager decided to start a journal. Her first entry listed a number of things she believed. "I believe," wrote the precocious teenager,

> (a) That there is no personal god or life after death (b) That the most desirable thing in the world is freedom to be true to oneself, i.e., Honesty (c) That the only difference between human beings is intelligence (d) That the only criterion of an action is its ultimate effect on making the individual happy or unhappy.

The year was 1947 and the young woman was Susan Sontag. She would go on to keep a journal until the last few years of her life. By the time of her death by blood cancer in 2004, she had filled nearly one hundred notebooks. She carefully kept them in chronological order in a walk-in closet in her bedroom along with other personal items such as photographs of her family and mementos from her childhood. To her son, David Rieff, was left the unenviable task of deciding whether they should be published.

According to Rieff, his mother died without leaving specific instructions about what to do with the journals. "The sole conversation I ever had with my mother about them," writes Rieff, "was when she first fell ill and had not yet rekindled her own belief that she would survive her blood cancer as she had the two previous cancers she had suffered in her lifetime." The conversation, states Rieff, "consisted of a single, whispered sentence: 'You know where the diaries are.'" There was, however, no indication as to what he should do with them.

Journals are cut from the same cloth as letters. And just as we can now imagine the last great writer to correspond with lovers and friends exclusively by letter, so too can we imagine a time when the habit of writing down with pen and paper our most private thoughts going the way of the telegraph and the typewriter.

My own leading candidate for the last writer to correspond exclusively by letter is William Gaddis, whose remarkable correspondence by letter was published in 2013. While there is still time for a trunk of letters from one of our remarkable contemporary writers to be unearthed from a closet or attic by a relative, it seems unlikely because most notable writers today have already settled the fate of their journals, correspondence, and unpublished manuscripts. Sontag too was no different in this regard.

Her son tells us that while she was still well, his mother sold her papers to the University of California at Los Angeles library, where they would go upon her death. These papers were to include her journals. As part of the UCLA archive, Sontag believed the contract she signed with the university library would not restrict access to them. Thus, her son concluded, "Either I would organize [her journals] and present them or someone else would." "It seemed better," concluded Rieff, "to go forward."

But he also indicates that he still had some "misgivings" about publishing them. "To say that these diaries are self-revelatory," comments Rieff, "is a drastic understatement." He then explains why:

> I have chosen to include a lot of my mother's very severe judgments. She was a great "judger." But to expose that quality in her—and these diaries are replete with exposures— is inevitably to invite the reader to judge *her*. One of the principle dilemmas in all this has been that, at least in her later life, my mother was not a very self-revealing person. In particular, she avoided to the extent she could, without denying it, any discussion of her own homosexuality or any

acknowledgement of her own ambition. So my decision certainly violates her privacy. There is no other way of describing it fairly.

But, in all fairness to Rieff, his mother wrote extensively and directly in her journals about her sexuality. Given that they were to be placed in a public university archive without any restrictions regarding access, short of destroying the journals or not turning them over to UCLA, her private life and thoughts—both severe and sensitive—were destined to reach an audience outside of their sanctuary in her closet. For that matter, a few years before her death, she was forced to come out regarding her sexuality by two biographers who held firm on "outing" her in spite of her wishes to remain publicly silent on the matter.

"My mother's was, I think," remarks Rieff, "a nineteenth-century consciousness, and the self-absorption of these journals has something of the tone of those great, selfish 'accomplishers.'" He also remarks in passing how this consciousness as manifested through journal writing began to shift in her final years "when her delight in the computer and in e-mail seems to have curbed her interest in diary keeping."

Keeping a journal for one's entire life beginning at the age of fourteen cannot help but determine one's consciousness. In 1947, aside from a typewriter, the pen was the only way for a young writer to think through their life in writing. Journal writing is a path that many great writers had taken before her and through which many began their writing life. "I write to define myself," says Sontag in an undated entry probably from early 1962. Writing is "an act of self-creation," she continues, "part of [the] process of becoming—In a dialogue with myself, with writers I admire living and dead, with ideal readers . . . Because it gives me pleasure."

"The writer," says Sontag in an entry on December 3, 1961, "must be four people: 1) The nut, the obsédé; 2) The moron; 3) The stylist; 4) The critic. 1 supplies the material; 2 lets it come out; 3 is taste; 4 is intelligence. A great writer has all 4—but you can still be a good writer with only 1 and 2; they're all most important."

A journal is a place where ideas are incubated and writers create themselves. And in some cases, writer's journals even eclipse in power their "official" writings. A good example of this are the journals of Ralph Waldo Emerson, which clearly surpass his essays in philosophical power.

In the case of Susan Sontag, while only two of the projected three volumes of her journals and notebooks are now available (*Reborn, Journals & Notebooks, 1947-1963* [2008] and *As Consciousness Is Harnessed to Flesh, Journals & Notebooks, 1964-1980* [2012]), the shaping forces of her mind and its ideas are on full display in these journals. As with Emerson's journals, Sontag's exhibit a rawness and vitality not possible in writing for public consumption. Wise beyond her years, the teenage Sontag writes in her journal, "Ideas disturb the levelness of life" (April 13, 1948). Indeed, it is hard too for the reader privileged to observe her life and ideas take shape in these journals to not experience a similar disturbance in their own life while reading them.

&

"Surely," writes Roland Barthes, "there is no longer a single adolescent who has this fantasy: *to be a writer!*" "Imagine," he continues, "wanting to copy not the works but the practices of any contemporary—his way of strolling through the world, a notebook in his pocket and a phrase in his head."

Barthes is speaking here not about the "art of writing," viz., copying works, but rather the "art of life," viz., copying the *life practices* of the writer.

These lines are from his wonderful postmodern autobiography, *Roland Barthes by Roland Barthes* (1975). It would be a work, which along with *The Pleasure of the Text* (1973), would establish him late in his career as an unapologetic proponent of hedonism.

"Being a hedonist (since he regards himself as one)," confesses Barthes in his autobiography, "he seeks a state which is, really, comfort." His adoption of hedonism was done with a full awareness that he stood alone among the literary theorists and philosophers of his time (and now ours) in his explicit engagement with the hedonic tradition.

In a parenthetical comment, Barthes asks "[W]ho today would call himself a hedonist with a straight face?" "[I]t can embarrass the text's return to morality, to truth: it is an oblique, a drag anchor, so to speak, without which the theory of the text would revert to a centered system, a philosophy of meaning." Barthes is familiar with the long history of hedonism in philosophy, and calls upon it with the aim of becoming its newest chapter. Hedonism is "a very old tradition," comments Barthes, which "has been repressed by nearly every philosophy; we find it defended only by marginal figures, Sade, Fourier; for Nietzsche, hedonism is a pessimism."

For critics and readers of Barthes, the adoption of hedonism appeared to be a new development in his thought. Indeed, Barthes himself notes in his autobiography that this turn to "morality" is the fifth genre of writing to date in which he has engaged. However, I would offer that Barthes was a hedonist long before he ostensibly "turned" to it in *The Pleasure of the Text* and *Roland Barthes by Roland Barthes*.

Like Sontag, whose journals and notebooks stand as a working catalogue of the pleasures in her life, and whose first journal entry, "That the only criterion of an action is its ultimate effect on making the individual happy or unhappy," indicates her own early commitment to hedonism, Barthes was a lifelong hedonist whose autobiography maps out the various sources of pleasure in his own life: in it, he discusses the pleasure of kissing, embracing, inserting ("Is there not a kind of voluptuous pleasure in inserting"), the endoxal products of mass culture, writing beginnings/fragments ("he tends to multiply this pleasure: that is why he writes fragments"), the Political ("I believe I understand that the Political pleases me as a *Sadean* text and displeases me as a *Sadistic* text"), Haiku, sexy sentences, ideology, contrary opinions of whether he is a Sorbonne professor, calculation, writing, etymology, piano playing, perversion ("in this case, that of the two H.'s: homosexuality and hashish"), friends, fantasizing—and his displeasure of translation, foreign literature, and foreign languages ("little taste for foreign literature, constant pessimism with regard to translation") and dreaming ("Dreaming [whether nicely or nastily] is insipid").

At one point, Barthes even explicitly confronts and lists, without explanations, many of the things he likes and dislikes:

> *I like:* salad, cinnamon, cheese, pimento, marzipan, the smell of new-cut hay (why doesn't someone with a "nose" make such a perfume), roses, peonies, lavender, champagne, loosely held political convictions, Glenn Gould, too-cold

19

beer, flat pillows, toast, Havana cigars, Handel, slow walks, pears, white peaches, cherries, colors, watches, all kinds of writing pens, desserts, unrefined salt, realistic novels, the piano, coffee, Pollock, Twombly, all romantic music, Sartre, Brecht, Verne, Fourier, Eisenstein, trains, Médoc wine, having change, *Bouvard and Pécuchet,* walking in sandals on the lanes of southwest France, the bend of the Adour seen from Doctor L. 's house, the Marx Brothers, the mountains at seven in the morning leaving Salamanca, etc.

I don't like: white Pomeranians, women in slacks, geraniums, strawberries, the harpsichord, Miró, tautologies, animated cartoons, Arthur Rubinstein, villas, the afternoon, Satie, Bartók, Vivaldi, telephoning, children's choruses, Chopin's concertos, Burgundian branles and Renaissance dances, the organ, Marc-Antoine Charpentier, his trumpets and kettledrums, the politico-sexual, scenes, initiatives, fidelity, spontaneity, evenings with people I don't know, etc.

The field of pleasure established by Barthes in *Roland Barthes by Roland Barthes* is vast, diverse, and idiosyncratic.

Like Sontag, however, Barthes's journals and notebooks were not published during his lifetime. And while both found value in the practice of journal writing, Barthes's theoretical connection with journal writing was deeper than that of most writers including Sontag. For him, the writer's journal is not merely an incubation tray for ideas. Rather, the "fragmentary" writing style of journals and notebooks cuts to the very character of his writing and thinking in general.

"I have the illusion to suppose," writes Barthes, "that by breaking up my discourse I cease to discourse in terms of the imaginary about myself, attenuating the risk of transcendence; but since the fragment (haiku, maxim, *pensée*, journal entry) is *finally* a rhetorical genre and since rhetoric is that layer of language which best presents itself to interpretation, by supposing I disperse myself I merely return, quite docilely, to the bed of the imaginary." In other words, the fragmentary writing style of his books pushes him in closer affinity to journal writing. "With the alibi of a pulverized discourse, a dissertation destroyed, one arrives at the regular practice of the fragment; then from the fragment one slips to the 'journal.'" "At which point," asks Barthes in his autobiography, "is not the point of all this to entitle oneself to write a 'journal?'" "Am I not justified in considering everything I have written as a clandestine and stubborn effort to bring to light again, someday, quite freely, the theme of the Gidean 'journal?'"

The problem though for Barthes was that he also thought that the autobiographical journal was a relic from the past—and "is, nowadays, discredited." However, "in the sixteenth century, when they were beginning to be written, without repugnance they were called a *diary: diarrhea* . . . ." Barthes is a writer who by his own admission is against journal writing, but who also prompts us to consider *everything* that he has written as a form of journal writing.

The key though to understanding his thoughts on journal writing is found in the work of André Gide. The very same year that Sontag started writing her own journal, Gide was awarded the Nobel Prize in Literature. What then happened to the writer's journal between 1947 and 1975 that might have led Barthes to "discredit" journal writing? And, more importantly, is the writer's journal still not credible today?

ॐ

André Gide sparked in Roland Barthes the desire to write. He was also there for Sontag upon her birth as a writer—and is arguably the sole source of her desire to keep a journal for the entirety of her life.

Sontag tells us that she read one of the four volumes of Gide's journals on "the same day I acquired it." "I should have read it much more slowly and I must re-read it many times," writes the fifteen-year-old Sontag. "Gide and I have attained such perfect intellectual communion that I experience the appropriate labor pains for every thought he gives birth to!" "Thus I do not think: 'How marvelously lucid this is!—but: 'Stop! I cannot think this fast! Or rather I cannot grow this fast!"

In 1948, when Sontag tells us she was reading Gide, he was at the height of his international reputation. It is widely acknowledged that his journals are his greatest achievement as a writer, and were a primary reason he was awarded the Nobel Prize. Unlike both Sontag and Barthes, who did not publish anything from their journals during their lifetime, Gide's journals appeared during his lifetime in both

21

periodicals and book form. In 1939, a one-volume Pléiade edition of his journals from 1889 to 1939 was published. Previously, the entirety of his journal from 1889 to 1932 was available in a complete edition of his works. Moreover, Gide continued to keep a journal even after complete editions of his journals were published in the 1930s—and these too were published.

Gide began keeping a journal at the age of eighteen or nineteen. Though he did not intend to publish his journals, he had already decided to become a writer. The volume of Gide's journals that the teenage Sontag was reading was published in English on May 24, 1948 and covered the years 1914 to 1927. "For, I am not only reading this book," writes Sontag, "but creating it myself, and this unique and enormous experience has purged my mind of much of the confusion and sterility that has clogged it all these horrible months." One form of sterility these journals are particularly good at unclogging is sexual sterility.

In his journals, Gide speaks openly about his homosexuality and that of his friends. In the volume that Sontag read at fifteen, Gide writes "I call a *pederast* the man who, as the word indicates, falls in love with young boys." "The pederasts," he continues, "of whom I am one (why cannot I say this quite simply, without your immediately claiming to see a brag in my confession?), are much rarer" than the sodomites, "the man whose desire is addressed to mature men." These frank journal entries from February of 1918 also include the entry, "Had Socrates and Plato not loved young men, what a pity for Greece, what a pity for the whole world."

And, regarding his friend Marcel Proust, for example, with whom he had spent an hour on the evening May 14, 1921, he writes in his journal the next day, "as soon as I arrived" he began "to talk of homosexuality." "Far from denying or hiding his homosexuality," comments Gide, "he [Proust] exhibits it, and I could almost say boasts of it."

Gide said in 1931 that he hoped that the publication of his journals would help prevent misinterpretation of his novels and other writings, which he thought were often misunderstood. He also believed that he was writing for posterity. While Gide's own literary star has descended quite a bit since its apex in 1947, his influence on a generation of writers that include Roland Barthes and Susan Sontag is undeniable.

Gide influenced Barthes's fragmentary writing style. In fact, one of Barthes earliest publications is a 1942 essay entitled "On Gide and His Journal." It is also the first article in *A Barthes Reader* (1982), which is edited with an introduction by Susan Sontag. "As it happens," writes Sontag in her introduction, "the first essay Barthes ever published celebrates the model consciousness he found in the *Journal* of André Gide, and what turned out to be the last essay published before he died ["Deliberation" (1979)] offers Barthes's musings on his own journal-keeping." The epigraph to this chapter comes from Barthes's last essay.

Of the influence of Gide on his own writing style, Barthes writes in his autobiography, "His first, or nearly first text (1942) consists of fragments; this choice is then justified in the Gidean manner 'because incoherence is preferable to a distorting order.' Since then, as a matter of fact, he has never stopped writing in brief bursts: the brief scenes of *Mythologies*, the articles and prefaces of *Critical Essays*, the lexias of *S/Z*, the fragments of the second essay on Sade in *Sade, Fourier, Loyola* and of *The Pleasure of the Text.*"

But Gide represents more than just a style of writing for Barthes—he is, as Barthes says in his autobiography, literally his *Abgrund*:

> One of his first articles (1942) concerned Gide's *Journal;* the writing of another *"En Grèce"* (1944), was evidently imitated from [Gide's] *Les Nourritures terrestres.* And Gide occupied a great place in his early reading: a diagonal cross-breed of Alsace and Gascony, as Gide was of Normandy and Languedoc, Protestant, having a taste for "letters" and fond of playing the piano, without counting the rest—how could he have failed to recognize himself, to desire himself in this writer? The Gidean *Abgrund*, the Gidean core, unchanging, still forms in my head a stubborn swarm. Gide is my original language, my *Ursuppe*, my literary soup.

23

Going back to Barthes' early essay on Gide, we learn a bit more about the early influence of Gide on him. Barthes here calls Gide "another Montaigne," presumably because both are skeptics that question all values, and both revel in their uncertainties and inconsistencies. Barthes is also drawn to Gide because of his break from conventional morality.

For Gide, a trip to North Africa in 1893 and 1894 brought him into contact with the radically different moral standards of the Arab world that helped liberate him from Victorian conventions. This intellectual revolt also brought Gide to a growing awareness of his homosexuality, where he was aided by a famous literary mentor, Oscar Wilde.

When the Nobel Prize organization announced his award for literature in 1947, they described it as grounded in "never resolved tensions between a strict artistic discipline, a puritanical moralism, and the desire for unlimited sensual indulgence and abandonment of life." Barthes writes in his early essay on Gide that his work comprises "a net of which no mesh can be dropped," and that it is futile to try to divide it up chronologically or methodologically. "It almost requires to be read in the fashion of certain Bibles," comments Barthes.

In his autobiography, Barthes says there are two Gides: one imagined and one actual. "For what the fantasy imposes is the writer as we can see him in his private diary, *the writer minus his work*: supreme form of the sacred: the mark and the void." Who was the Gide we see in his journal? For that matter, who was the Barthes we see in his private diary? Or the Sontag we see in her private journal?

For Gide, his journal was the place where he could "revel in his contradictions," where "I am never," rather "I become." Sontag, perhaps inspired by Gide, wrote in her own journal, "To write you have to allow yourself to be the person you don't want to be (of all the people you are)" (August 13, 1961). And Barthes, whose books are paradoxically perhaps the best example of his journal writing, sadly, spoke eloquently of his lifelong struggles with boredom in his own private writings including his letters and journals. In a letter to a friend on August 31, 1932, a sixteen-year-old Barthes describes himself as a "decidedly boring fellow," who fears that he will "bore" his friend. And then, on September 17, 1979, less than a year before his untimely death on March 26, 1980, Barthes writes in his own journal, after some attempts at flirting, "ultimately, I'm bored."

そ

The writer's journal today is not what it used to be. Its high point in twentieth-century world literature was reached by Gide. If Gide took the writer's journal out of the closet of world literature, then writers who followed in his footsteps such as Barthes and Sontag both literally and figuratively put it back in the closet. Though both followed Gide's lead in openly discussing their sexuality in their journals, neither chose to publish their journals during their lifetime. Barthes even went so far as to describe the writer's journal as a discredited form of writing.

As a private sanctuary for writers, there is still no better habit for a young writer to acquire than keeping a journal. However, the risk of being defined as a writer and judged as a human being is always the risk of offering these private writings to the public. For some, like Gide, the desire to make this public offering was strong. For others, like Sontag and Barthes, they preferred to let their books speak for them—and keep the pleasure (and pain) of journal writing a private one in their otherwise very public lives.

Today there are now many more technologically advanced ways to see a *writer minus her work*. Nonetheless, even if journal writing is still a discredited practice, the opportunity to view a favorite writer's journal or notebook is not. Reading emails cannot replace or simulate the singular and cherished experience of reading the diary of a writer—even if that writer, like Barthes, doubts the value of what they have written.

25

3 | INDUSTRIAL DISEASE

"As Gregor Samsa awoke one morning from uneasy dreams he found himself transformed in his bed into a gigantic insect .... What has happened to me? He thought. It was no dream."

—Franz Kafka, *The Metamorphosis* (1915)

Amazon has spread to every corner of the publishing industry in America. And everyone knows it is an industrial disease.

For those in the traditional publishing industry, Amazon is a contagion that is one of the primary sources of the decline of an industry that has been trending downward ever since the dawn of digital books. Not only has Amazon cornered the market on book sales and distribution, it is also now a rising power in the book publishing business.

If this were not enough, it also collects user data on your purchasing and reading habits. Recently, it went even further by offering Amazon shoppers a $10 dollar credit in exchange for handing over their browser data. With this additional data, the company now knows not only what you purchase from its online store and your reading habits through its ebook services, but also, for customers who download the Amazon Assistant app to their browser, it knows the search terms and keystrokes which led to your purchase of items on the internet.

For the traditional publishing industry, these and other moves by Amazon are like a gigantic insect that crawls up on your plate at dinnertime rendering your meal inedible. Scream all you want, but it's not going to change anything. The traditional publishing industry has met in Amazon a formidable and destructive competitor.

While I am no fan of traditional publishing today, a world where the market is all, and where a handful of publishing corporations now enjoy market hegemony, at least traditional publishing only knew your purchasing and reading behavior

27

indirectly and imprecisely. Amazon knows exactly *what* you purchase and, if it was an ebook, *how* you read it. And they are becoming better by the year at reading you in order to maximize their ability to sell you more products.

Amazon is the world's largest public company with an estimated 550 million retail items on its website. In addition, it has data on billions of customer transactions including information on every purchase you have ever made on Amazon. They have perfected the science of using this data to improve their customer targeting. It is not inconceivable in the future that when you log on to Amazon, it will provide you suggestions for products tailored to your precise spending range and product interests. One can even imagine a day when Amazon provides you with books that are specifically generated to meet your reading expectations regarding style, content, and form.

The first step toward this though requires Amazon to get into the book publishing business, which is something it has already begun. To date, Amazon Publishing has 15 imprints in the U.S. and publishes everything from translations to romance novels, and it is growing fast. In 2009 Amazon published 373 titles, whereas in 2017 they published 1,231 titles. Moreover, these books seem to be selling—and some of them selling big.

One author, Mark Sullivan, who wrote a military saga that was rejected by eight New York publishers, received a low five-figure advance for his book from Amazon Publishing. Immediately upon publication, it had 300,000 downloads and to date has sold more than 1.5 million copies. It was ranked by USA Today as the 56th best-selling book of 2018.

Sales figures like this are possible because Amazon can promote these non-traditionally published books through its ebook subscription services, Amazon First Reads and Kindle Unlimited, which serve an estimated 10 million customers. As of 2019, 72% of all adult new book sales online and 49% of all new book sales by unit are through Amazon. But the potential market for their books is even larger because Amazon has over 100 million Amazon Prime members world-wide, who are allowed to select one Amazon First Reads book a month at no cost. Kindle Unlimited is an ebook subscription service that had as of 2018 an estimated 4.6 million subscribers, who for $9.99 a month can select as many as 10 books at a time—and each book that is downloaded through this service counts as a sale.

Publishing industry experts are reeling though because through these ebook services, Amazon Publishing and Amazon self-published books are prominently displayed to their users. This is a cruel stroke of irony for a book industry that used to enjoy the same prominence of display through arrangements with the chain bookstores of the late twentieth-century. Prominent display in Amazon First Reads and Kindle Unlimited is akin to the "book monsters" (to wit, a large display for a new book) that used to attack you when you walked into a chain bookstore such as Borders or B. Dalton.

Amazon's move into non-traditional publishing is a serious competitive challenge for the publishing industry and is making it much more difficult for this industry to continue with business as usual. If the devastating effects of Amazon on the traditional publishing industry continue, not only will the state of publishing in the U.S. be forever changed, so too will the business of books across the world. Whether it is for the better depends on how much you are willing to sacrifice your privacy for book purchasing convenience and lower price points.

᠁

What do you do though when an industry to which authors and readers have entrusted their hopes and dreams has become diseased? What do you do when your beliefs about the publishing world have become tainted by a contagion? When self-publishing has become the dominant force in publishing? These are questions Amazon raises for everyone who works within and enjoys the fruits of the publishing industry.

Most would revile in disgust and throw away their meal if they found a gigantic insect on their plate. If they still retained an appetite, rather than eat their meal, they might just ask for another to be brought out to them. But in the case of a contagion like Amazon in the publishing industry, what would we throw away? Just the parts of the industry that have come to be corrupted by Amazon? If so, how do we separate them from the uncorrupted parts? Do we even know anymore what buying books and reading them uncorrupted by Amazon looks like? Or how publishing would function in the digital age without Amazon? Isn't neoliberal habitus so entrenched in the book production and sales industry that it is not possible to perceive the book world without it? After all, doesn't Amazon spoil *all* aspects

29

of the publishing industry, and not just parts of it?

For some, rejecting the publishing industry corrupted by Amazon is tantamount to asking for an uncorrupted version of it. But even so, when we send it back to the publishing industry for a new plate, what version of the publishing industry do we want? One that goes back to the future of the publishing industry, that is, to a state of it *before* it became corrupted by Amazon or to an entirely new version of it, that is, a version of the publishing industry that has not yet materialized?

My own preference leans toward the latter, to a publishing industry to come forged out of twenty-first-century life and experience. One untainted by the neoliberal contagion and supportive of democratic values, critical exchange, and distributive justice as well as the advancement of truth, knowledge, and beauty. I envision this to be a publishing world where book production and reading across the globe takes on a character less driven by market domination and more driven by cosmopolitanism and humanitarianism. This is a version of biotheoretical thinking that I term *bibliotheory*.

But plenty of folks in traditional corporate publishing would be satisfied to just go back to the way things were at some point last century before the rise of Amazon. That is, to bring back the good ol' days of the twentieth-century corporate publishing industry, rather than strive toward a post-neoliberal publishing world tempered by cosmopolitan and humanitarian concerns.

Still, our dreams notwithstanding, neither of these things are what happens when we identify Amazon as a contagion. While we may wish for a new plate of the publishing industry, we're still stuck with the one that Amazon is feeding us. The restoration of the pre-Amazon publishing world or the arrival of the post-Amazon cannot be fulfilled on short notice. To think otherwise is a pipe dream. Amazon is here to stay, growing larger and more powerful by the day—or, better yet, by the *data*.

While visions of working in a pre- or post-neoliberal publishing world may sustain us through the contagion, in point of fact, the contagion continues to spread and there is really not much we can do to alter its course. After discovery of publishing's contagion, don't be surprised if you are still reading and purchasing books through Amazon—albeit, perhaps, with a bitter taste in our mouth. It is a disgusting taste though one that is not always accompanied with a look of disgust. Many have found a spoonful of sugar to help the contagion go down. Namely, that sweetness found in the appreciation of books that are cheap, plentiful, and easy to purchase on Amazon.

Nonetheless, just because most of us participate in one way or another in Amazon's publishing juggernaut, which is now the mainstream of the book business, it does not make the publishing industry under late capitalism any less corrupted. We have just lowered our resistance to the contagion in order to get on with our meal—that is, to just get on with reading and enjoying the books that give value and meaning to our lives.

A starving person will not pass up a meal just because they find a gigantic insect in it. For that matter, some get so desperate for food that they choose to eat insects rather than go hungry. In the age of the Amazon contagion, we do not uncontaminate the publishing industry in order to function in it. Rather we make it palatable by altering in some way our own emotional response to the contagion. We have no choice in the matter, especially if the only alternative is book starvation, that is, to walk away from the world of books.

Creepy or gross as it may be, those of us who partake of this industrial disease are doing something akin to the person who eats their meal in spite of finding a bug in it. They have found a way to override their strong and immediate emotional repulsion to Amazon and get on with their life in the world of books. One would be hard pressed to find a better analogy for the emotional psychodynamics of Amazon in the twenty-first-century publishing industry.

For most, particularly those who work in the traditional publishing industry, Amazon's presence is a *negative* contagion. It is something that elicits emotional responses such as anger, sadness, and fear. But there is also a completely different response to their contamination of the publishing industry. Namely, to see it as a *positive* contagion or something that elicits emotional responses more akin to love and joy.

In order to view Amazon as a positive contamination, one would need to fully embrace it as an operational paradigm for the book industry. One would have to hold the view that a gigantic insect on the plate of the publishing industry *is a good thing*, something that elicits the opposite of a fearful, angry, or sad reaction. In fact,

31

on such a view, the presence of no number of insects or any other vermin on their meal would get them to change their positive outlook of Amazon's industrial disease. As a positive contagion, the intensification of Amazon's practices and policies are joyful events.

From the positive perspective on contagion, Amazon's role in the publishing industry is not to *destroy* it, but rather to restore it and bring it back to health. Their infestation of the publishing industry aims both to transform publishing to comport better in a system of value where anything and everything can and should be sold or plundered for profit, and to reshape publishing for a world structured by equations and driven by numbers.

Moreover, as a positive contamination, Amazon is only concerned with books and literature so long as they maximize the ends of capital. Its aim is to eat through whatever is put on its plate: books, bolts, bowling balls, it doesn't matter. They are all interchangeable commodities valued only on the basis of their comparative marketability and profit margin among the 550 million or so items in their inventory. The publishing industry is as good a target as any for decimation and domination because it lends itself well (as the publishing house mergers of the twentieth-century have amply demonstrated) to market monopolization.

Gigantic insects aside though, personality and social psychology provides some interesting insight on the power of these two very different contagions in the lives of readers and writers. From their perspective, there is a general bias toward negativity rather than positivity. In terms of contagion, this means that negative contagions *are more powerful* than positive ones. Research has shown that negativity bias and domination is based both on experience and innate predispositions. But there is other evidence as well to our predisposition toward negativity.

One of my favorite pieces of non-scientific evidence for negativity bias was a study on possession in Western and non-Western religions. It concluded that on the one hand, it is a relatively brief and easy affair to be become possessed by a malevolent demonic force, whereas the ritual of exorcism is by comparison a painstaking and prolonged one. On the other hand, there is a very long trajectory of positive moral acts required to be deemed "holy" or "saintly," but there is by comparison a very short moral trajectory to become compromised, that is, it only takes one or a few immoral deeds.

Indeed, *possession* of the publishing world by Amazon was a relatively brief and easy affair, particularly when compared against the backdrop of the long history of publishing both in itself and as an industry. And if the psychologists are right, it is going to be a long process to exorcise this contagion from the publishing world.

On the flip side, as a positive contagion, let's hope that Amazon continues to be a hard sell within the publishing world and is as easily challengeable as the process of "becoming 'saintly.'" There is nothing holy or saintly about Amazon, particularly from the position of those who try to compete with it in the book business.

Regarding Amazon as a contagion allows us to understand better how it has grown so quickly and why it will be so difficult to stop. The images of Amazon as an industrial disease that is contaminating the publishing world or as a malevolent demonic force that is possessing publishing may be disgusting or disturbing ones, but they are nonetheless effective ones.

Perhaps though the power of Amazon as a negative contagion is more simply exemplified through recalling the Russian adage about tar and honey. "A spoonful of tar can spoil a barrel of honey," says the adage, "but a spoonful of honey does nothing for a barrel of tar." Like the spoonful of tar that is spoiling the barrel of honey, Amazon is contaminating the publishing world. And though the publishing industry has never been the land of milk and honey, it has also never been a barrel of tar. For many, a spoonful of Amazon long ago spoiled publishing and its industry. What we are left with today is more like a barrel of tar than a barrel of honey.

These negative images pave the way for consideration not only of the relative power of Amazon, but also how this power is constituted and spread by our emotional reactions to it in the publishing industry. Understanding why and how emotional contagion works in publishing will also provide us with some clues as to how to move beyond one of its most extreme neoliberal manifestations.

33

❧

If you enjoy being read as much as you enjoy reading, then the Amazon contagion is more like a drop of honey in a barrel of tar.

But if you would rather have a human rather than an algorithm help you to navigate the world of books, then Amazon is a spoonful of tar in the honey barrel of books and reading.

Sorry if the bugs grossed you out. But Amazon is a gross business. Plus, one of the most memorable images from world literature is Kafka's gigantic insect. Amazon's *transformation* of the publishing industry in America calls for a similarly disgusting image. Amazon is an industrial disease for the book business—one that most of us have caught and grapple with daily.

4 | THE SPEED OF PUBLISHING

SIDE 1 / SLOW PUBLISHING

Writing is a slow process. And the traditional publishing process is often an even slower one.

What writer has not heard this tune? The grooves of the publishing world's "Slow Side" have been on continuous play for a very, very long time. It is Side One of an album that until very recently has been played as if it were the only side.

The Slow Side opens with a literary agent. In the U.S. alone, there are more than 1,000 literary agents with many of them specializing in a particular area or subarea of writing including fiction, nonfiction, children's, picture, middle grade, young adult, Christian, African-American, and boutique. If you do not have a literary agent to pitch and sell your work, then the process of finding one can be a time consuming and frustrating one.

Many suggest that those seeking an agent submit multiple and simultaneous query letters, especially if your goal is to find *the best* person and not just *a* person. The Associated Writing Programs (AWP) recently offered to help aspiring writers to find an agent by facilitating the submission of short samples of member's work to multiple literary agencies. If one or more of these agencies saw potential in your work, they would then schedule a meeting with you at the AWP conference to discuss the possibility of representing you to acquisitions editors.

Finding a literary agent though is just the first tune on the Slow Side of publishing. Once you have an agent, you then need to reach some type of an agreement on your book proposal. On the short end of the time spectrum, this might take anywhere from one to four months; on the long end, there are stories of agents working with authors in excess of two years on proposals.

This second cut on the Slow Side of publishing shares a resemblance with the second cut on vinyl albums. Just as the second cut on Side One is often the best tune on an album, so too must your proposal be strong in order to better your chances of landing a book contract—let alone a lucrative one. After your proposal is completed, your agent will pitch your project to various editors in the hope of selling it to them. But again, like the timeline for developing a proposal, landing a book contract can take anywhere from one month to two years for a successful result.

Now that you have an editor who is going to work on your project with you, you will need to negotiate the details of your book contract. Depending on the amount of the advance and other important details, this can be wrapped up in a couple of weeks or can drag on for months. Good news though is that most authors will move ahead with working on their final manuscript while contract details are getting sorted out. If the manuscript is complete, then it will be sent to your editor to read, which usually takes about two months. However, if the manuscript is not complete, then it may be due to the press up to eighteen months after the contract is signed.

Editors usually expect some revisions for your manuscript, which might take you anywhere from a week to a month. In the case that extensive revisions are required, then a month might become months, but hopefully not much longer. The next stage of the process is getting your manuscript into galleys, which usually takes traditional publishers anywhere from four to six months after revisions. You are then given a few weeks to read over the galleys and make corrections. Once the galleys have been corrected, then your book is sent to a printer. Depending on the quality of the printer, you might have hard copies the next day or the next month. Finally, a month or two after it ships from the printer, your book will be available in bookstores for purchase.

I review the timeline for the traditional publication process in effort to *defamiliarize* a familiar process. In "Art as Technique" (1917), Viktor Shklovsky, argued that the purpose of art is to change our sensation of things from automatic to aesthetic:

> The purpose of art is to impart the sensation of things as they are perceived, and not as they are known. The technique of art is to make objects "unfamiliar," to make forms difficult, to increase the difficulty and length of perception, because the process of perception is an aesthetic end in itself and must be

prolonged. Art is a way of experiencing the artfulness of an object; the object is not important.

Our response to the traditional publication process *has* become automatic. From securing the services of a literary agent and working closely with an editor to the elements of book editing and design, the aesthetic is never far from the traditional publishing process. Is being a literary agent more of an art than a science? Same with book editing and design? Defamiliarizing the process of traditional book publishing encourages us to regard it as an aesthetic process. Moreover, when we increase the difficulty and length of perceiving it, we are compelled to regard the publishing process *itself* as an aesthetic object—and not just the object this process produces, that is to say, the book

One of the effects of the aestheticization of the traditional publishing process is to find art and beauty in it slowness. Slow cooking a book with a literary agent and an editor can take anywhere from nine months to nine years or more. We all know examples of both the shorter road and the longer one. While there are sometimes gasps when a writer announces at a reading that their book is the product of a ten-year process, more often than not, there is more empathy in the room than surprise.

Again, the slow process of writing and publishing is well known— and for some in the literary community, it is even a badge of honor. The slow tunes on Side One of *The Book Publishing Album* are all considered industry standards.

❧

SIDE 2 / FAST PUBLISHING

Writing is a fast process. And the non-traditional publishing process is often an even faster one.

This tune is coming to be played more and more in the publishing world. And though the grooves of the "Fast Side" of the publishing world are fairly recent ones, they are coming to be preferred by many authors to the well-worn grooves and standard tunes on the "Slow Side."

It's old news by now that the "Fast Side" of the publishing world began to be played more in earnest in 2007 when the Kindle Readers made electronic books a more viable option to printed ones. It is not that there were not ebooks before the Kindle Reader, it's just that this e-reader made reading them a whole lot easier. And just as the move from vinyl records (and 8-tracks, cassettes, and CDs) to digital files changed the music industry, so too did the move from printed to electronic books change the publishing industry.

But the backtracks of ebooks go even deeper if one calls upon the category *electronic literature*. If the history of print books (pbooks) is entwined with the evolution of Gutenberg's invention, then the history of electronic literature (and Side Two of *The Book Publishing Album*) is, in the words of N. Katherine Hayles from *Electronic Literature* (2008), "entwined with the evolution of digital computers as they shrank from the room-sized IBM 1401 machine . . . (sporting all of 4K memory) to the networked machine on [her] desktop, thousands of times more powerful and able to access massive amounts of information from around the world."

Moreover, for Hayles, the case for listening more closely (and often) to Side Two of *The Book Publishing Album* goes even deeper than just the evolution of digital computers (and e-readers):

> Literature in twenty-first century is computational . . . almost all print books are digital files before they become books; this is the form in which they are composed, edited, composited, and sent to the computerized machines that produce them as books. They should, then, properly be considered as electronic texts for which print is the output form.

The fastest cuts then on the Fast Side of *The Book Publishing Album* are those that are all digital. They are ebooks that have been composed, edited, composited, and read digitally. At the most extreme, these fast cuts have no connection with print—and from start to finish are completely paperless productions. But the speed differential here turns not just on the existential difference between analog and digital art, but also on the networks associated with slow publishing versus fast publishing.

Slow publishing in its purest form involves many people in addition to the author: an agent, an editor, a publisher, a compositor, a cover designer, a publicist, a printer, someone to warehouse your book; someone to deliver it to a bookstore; someone to shelf it and sell it at a bookstore; and so on. The slowness of slow publishing is grounded in the multifarious human agents that can only move as fast as the speed of muscle and mind.

By contrast, fast publishing in its purest form only involves an author. Non-traditional publishing affords the intrepid and entrepreneurial author the opportunity to perform *all* of the functions previously delegated among many individuals. Moreover, there are even some self-publishing companies that for a fee will even write your book for you.

While I can hear the authorial gasps at the thought of someone writing your book for you for a fee, this is not entirely unchartered territory. Ghost writing is quite normal in the traditional publishing industry. And ghostwriters are not difficult to find. For example, Jerry Payne, bills himself online as a "Trusted Professional – Memoir Ghostwriter – Writing Consultant – Award-winning author," with the capacity to ghostwrite "Memoir, Business, How-To, Sports, History, Self-Help, Inspirational, Politics."

"I'm an award-winning ghostwriter and I can take something from the stage of a mere idea floating around in your head all the way to a printed book available to the world on Amazon," writes Payne. "I've ghostwritten or edited over forty books for a wide range of clients and I know I can help you too." "Best of all, you'll get all the credit." "For most books, you can expect a fee of $55,000, which includes everything from writing/editing/proofreading, all the way to publishing and making sure your book is available on Amazon and elsewhere. I'll even throw in the first 25 copies for free."

But the fast publishing of the future will eventually have the capacity to cut out Author's Guild members like Payne. First, there is the prospect of algorithms generating personalized fiction based on data from your Amazon reading habits. Second, folks like Payne who craft your material into a readable memoir will eventually be replaced by computer programs designed to serve the same function, albeit probably better and surely for a lower cost. In the future, therefore, the blinding speed of fast publishing will ultimately be grounded in a form of non-human agency whose speed is only limited by its digital processing and transmission capacities.

Fast publishing though is not just about computer-generated writing or electronic literature or ghostwriters-for-hire. It is also an emerging story about authors becoming less dependent upon the slowness of traditional publishing, and opting instead to become one of the speed freaks of the non-traditional publishing world. The need for speed though in the fast publishing world for authors that try to make a career here is determined by economics, not aesthetics. In short, the need to write faster is based on a desire to generate more revenue by publishing more writing—and not say the pursuit of some literary aesthetic ideal.

Take for example, fast publishing author I. T. Lucas. According to her personal website, Lucas is the "Internationally Bestselling Author" of two series of books: The Children of the Gods Series, which currently has 40 titles including *Dark Dream's Temptation* (2019) and *Dark Prince's Dilemma* (2019); and the Perfect Match Series, which currently has 3 titles including *Captain's Conquest* (2019). The exact publication dates of these three titles from 2019 are in order March 23, July 27, and July 13. But there is even more: over the course of three years, Lucas has published *twenty-one* full-length novels—and says that she works twelve hours a day, seven days a week.

Captain's Conquest, for example, is a one-hundred-and-fifty-eight-page novel about a romance between Gregg and Alicia. "Working as a Starbucks barista, Alicia fends off flirting all day long, but none of the guys are as charming and sexy as Gregg," reads the book description. "His frequent visits are the highlight of her day," it continues, "but since he's never asked her out, she assumes he's taken." "Besides, between a day job and a budding music career, she has no time to start a new relationship. This until Gregg makes her an offer she can't refuse—a gift certificate to the virtual fantasy fulfillment service everyone is talking about. As a huge Star Trek fan, Alicia has a perfect match in mind—the captain of the Starship Enterprise."

As a Kindle Unlimited member, you can acquire *Captain's Conquest* through Amazon.com for no cost. Currently, it is ranked among Amazon Best Sellers as the #215 Paranormal Ghost Romance, the #273 Science Fiction Romance, and the #265 Psychic Romance. Considering that it is the product of fast publishing, that is, one of seven novels Lucas produces on average *per year*, these sales figures too read like a science fiction romance. But as fast as Lucas writes and publishes, there are folks that are even faster.

Lea Robinson and Melissa King have teamed up to produce more than one hundred romance novels on Amazon *in just three years*. Writing together under the pen name Alexa Riley, they publish around three romance novels a month. Every day each of them tries to write 3,000 words of romance fiction—and it appears that they are succeeding.

The non-traditional publishing process has not only accelerated the publication process, but because the more you write, the more you make, it has also accelerated the writing process.

So much for the maxim "Writing is a slow process."

❧

BONUS TRACK

Kindle Direct Publishing allows authors like Lucas and Riley to directly upload their self-published books. And services like Kindle Unlimited allow their readers to feast at a digital buffet of romance fiction for very little cost. But how then do these authors get paid if Kindle Unlimited is not charging readers for the purchase of their books?

In the case of Lucas's *Captain's Conquest*, readers can either purchase a paperback for $8.99 or if they have a Kindle (but no subscription to Kindle Unlimited), they can purchase a Kindle version for $2.99 (which saves them $6.00 from the print price). But if they pay $9.99 a month, there is no cost to download the Kindle version of *Captain's Conquest*.

For all books self-published through Kindle Direct Publishing, if the book is priced between $2.99 and $9.99, authors earn a 70% royalty for all direct sales. The royalty rate however goes down to 35% for books priced below $2.99 and above $9.99. Still, this is not the only *or the best* way for Kindle Direct Publishing authors to make a profit off of their books. Rather, it is by designating themselves as Kindle Direct Publishing *Select* authors.

41

This means that as Kindle Direct Publishing Select authors, their self-published books *automatically* are put into Kindle Unlimited. Again, this means that readers can read them for no cost other than their subscription fee to Kindle Unlimited (in the same way that viewers can view films on Netflix). It also means that their title is available for free to Amazon Prime members, who are allowed to borrow one Kindle Owners' Lending Library book a month for free.

What happens then is that Amazon keeps data on the number of pages read (or viewed) each month for each particular book and author. At the end of the month, Amazon then divides a pot of money it sets aside for Kindle Direct Publishing Select authors based on the number of pages read from their books through Kindle Unlimited and Amazon Prime's Kindle Owner's Lending Library program. It comes to about one-half penny per page.

But there is also a *bonus track.*

Amazon awards tens of thousands of dollars of *bonus pay* to its most read Kindle Direct Publishing Select authors. This means that these self-published authors have a potential source of revenue in addition to the income they receive from both direct sales of their books (royalties), and direct page views in Kindle Unlimited and Amazon Prime's Kindle Owner's Lending Library program.

The motivation then to produce seven novels a year or three novels a month is to both maximize direct sales and page views, but also to secure a bonus for being a most read author. More books produced per year means more pages available for viewing. And the faster these books can be produced *and read*, the faster the money comes in for their self-published authors.

Many authors today are avoiding the slowness of traditional publishing—and opting instead for the speediness of non-traditional publishing. The rise of self-publishing has greatly increased the speed of publishing and maybe even the speed of reading.

Nevertheless, the costs associated with readers and writers more often playing the Fast Side of *The Book Publishing Album* are still to be determined.

à.

ALBUM NOTE

Rod Stewart's *Atlantic Crossing* (1975) and *A Night on the Town* (1976) are albums where one side is labeled the "Fast Side" and the other side the "Slow Side"—and also ones where one side is often more worn out than the other.

5 | SUSPICIOUS MINDS

"We can't go on together with suspicious minds and we can't build our dreams on suspicious minds."

—Mark James, "Suspicious Minds" (1968), which in 1969 became Elvis Presley's last U.S. number one single

Suspicion might be prime fodder for songwriters. But is it the proper way for students to read books? There has been a heated debate of late over this very question with the fate of the humanities appearing to hang in the balance.

Back in the early 1970s, the philosopher Paul Ricoeur provided what has become the classic formulation of suspicious reading. In his book, *Freud and Philosophy: An Essay on Interpretation* (1970), Ricoeur proposed two general directions for interpretation. One direction seeks to "purify discourse of its excrescences, liquidate the idols, go from drunkenness to sobriety, realize our state of poverty once and for all." The other direction "use[s] the most 'nihilistic,' destructive, iconoclastic movement so as to *let speak* what once, what each time, was *said*, when meaning appeared anew, when meaning was its fullest." For Ricoeur, hermeneutics, the art and technique of interpretting texts, is "animated by this double motivation: willingness to suspect, willingness to listen; vow of rigor, vow of obedience," a "tension" and "extreme polarity" that is the "truest expression of our 'modernity.'"

One direction he calls the "school of reminiscence" and the other the "school of suspicion." If the aim of the school of reminiscence is the restoration of meaning, then the aim of its opposite, the school of suspicion, is the demystification of meaning. For Ricoeur, the three "masters" that dominate the school of suspicion are Karl Marx, Friedrich Nietzsche, and Sigmund Freud. Though their lines of thought are "seemingly mutually exclusive," "[a]ll three begin with suspicion concerning the illusions of consciousness, and then proceed to employ the stratagem of deciphering." Thus, for Ricoeur, "the *Genealogy of Morals* in Nietzsche's sense, the theory of ideologies in the Marxist sense, and the theory of ideals and illusions in Freud's sense represent three convergent procedures of demystification."

Now, fifty years after Ricoeur dubbed Marx, Nietzsche, and Freud as the masters of the hermeneutics of suspicion, some scholars are arguing that these masters and their theoretical legacies are at the root of the problems facing the humanities today. The shorthand way of terming their approach to interpretating texts and documents is the word *critique*—which is widely regarded as the *modus operandi* of the humanities. But if the humanities are indeed *in peril*, is it possible then to save them by simply rejecting critique, their *modus operandi*? This "conviction," writes Rita Felski in her book *The Limits of Critique* (2015), is one that is "shared by a growing number of scholars." For these "postcritique" scholars, continues Felski, rejecting critique and its "rhetoric of suspicious reading in literary studies and in the humanities and interpretive sciences generally" is the solution to the woes facing the humanities.

While Felski, who currently holds the William R. Kenan Jr. Professorship of English at the University of Virginia and is also Niels Bohr Professor at the University of Southern Denmark, recognizes the criticism that rejecting critique is tantamount to becoming a "pawn of neoliberal interests," she nonetheless tries to distance herself from the neoliberal agenda for the humanities by saying that her real motivation is elsewhere. Namely, it is "a desire to articulate a positive vision for humanistic thought in the face of growing skepticism about its value." But in spite of her claims to articulate a "positive vision" for the humanities, Felski does the opposite. The postcritique that she promotes has produced a virulent and highly destructive form of antitheory, if not also, anti-humanities.

In a relatively short period of time, Felski has become the poster professor for attempting to *unpopularize* theory and its use in the humanities. Her high profile and higher funded postcritique movement, initiated just a few years ago, is an effort to move beyond the critique not only of Marx, Nietzsche, and Freud, but also a discernable though complex line of thought that runs from Immanuel Kant to Theodor Adorno, Jürgen Habermas, and contemporary thinkers such as Terry Eagleton, Fredric Jameson, and many others who have successfully championed and promoted critique for the past two-hundred and fifty or so years.

Felski's postcritique was rewarded in the form of a $4.2 million grant in 2016 from the Danish National Research Foundation. A press release from the University of Virginia announcing the grant says that it stems from work done in *The Limits of Critique*, which "encouraged her fellow scholars to explore alternatives to increasingly predictable and formulaic styles of 'suspicious reading.'" Felski, continues the release, says

> literary scholars should spend less time looking behind a text for hidden causes and suspicious motives and more time placing themselves in front of it to reflect on what it suggests, unfolds or makes possible. What literary studies needs, she said, is less emphasis on "de" words—demystifying, debunking, deconstructing—and more emphasis on "re" words—literature's potential to remake, reshape and recharge perception.

Felski claims that she will use the grant to "develop new frameworks and methods for exploring the many social uses of literature," something she has already begun in her course, "Theories of Reading," where, "students first learn to become skeptical readers, drawing on ideas from Freud, Foucault or feminism to criticize the works of the canon or to challenge their assumptions of their favorite TV shows," and then learn "to reflect on why they love certain novels or movies and to develop more sophisticated vocabularies for describing and justifying these feelings."

Felski's comments here are important to note because they betray the basic parameters of her attack against theory. For her, theory has become "predicable and formulaic," and she aims to provide it with "new frameworks and methods." These new "frameworks and methods," aim to establish "more sophisticated vocabularies for describing and justifying" why we "love certain novels and movies"—and, of course, television shows. The question remains though whether Felski's "new frameworks and methods" are really against theory or simply a new and improved form of theory.

Arguably, Felski builds her postcritique on the foundation of the

47

success of efforts like Terry Eagleton's to demystify and popularize theory in books like *Literary Theory: An Introduction* (1983). But her effort to place "more emphasis on 're' words—literature's potential to remake, reshape and recharge perception" comes with a bit of irony, especially when we consider that Eagleton opens up *Literary Theory* with the statement, "If one wanted to put a date on the beginnings of the transformation which has overtaken literary theory this century, one could do worse than settle on 1917, the year the young Russian Formalist Viktor Shklovsky published his pioneering essay, 'Art as Device'"—a piece which introduces the concepts of defamiliarization, foregrounding, and estrangement, arguing that art is a means to make things real again, that is to say, it is a means of recharging our perception of things. Hence, from Shklovsky in 1917 to Felski a century later, literary theory has arguably come full circle back to its storied beginnings in recharging our perception of things.

Prior to Felski though the French sociologist Bruno Latour also waged war on critique in his infamous 2003 Stanford presidential lecture, "Why Has Critique Run Out of Steam? From Matters of Fact to Matters of Concern," which was published the following year in the journal *Critical Inquiry*. Addressing an audience of academics at the Stanford Humanities Center, Latour asked, "What has critique become when a French general, no, a marshal of critique, namely, Jean Baudrillard, claims in a published book that the Twin Towers destroyed themselves under their own weight, so to speak, undermined by the utter nihilism inherent in capitalism itself—as if the terrorist planes were pulled to suicide by the powerful attraction of this black hole of nothingness? What has become of critique when a book that claims that no plane ever crashed into the Pentagon can be a bestseller?"

Latour sees in works of critique, such as Baudrillard's, a hastening of the desire toward "*revisionism*." "Remember the good old days when revisionism arrived very late," asks Latour, "after the facts had been thoroughly established, decades after bodies of evidence had accumulated?" Now because of the legacy of critique, we have "instant revisionism," says Latour. The smoke of an event barely clears before there arise multiple conspiracy theories "revising the official account." This new phenomenon of *instant revisionism* adds "even more ruins to the ruins . . . even more smoke to the smoke."

But these are not even the final ruins of critique. Rather, for

Latour, it comes when nonacademics express more critique-driven statements than academics. He reminds us of the "good old days when university professors could look down on unsophisticated folks because those hillbillies naïvely believed in church, motherhood, and apple pie." Now it is the "unsophisticated folks" who look down on the "sophisticated" ones when it comes to critique. "What has become of critique when my neighbor in the little Bourbonnais village where I live looks down on me as someone hopelessly naïve because I believe that the United States had been attacked by terrorists?"

For Latour, Baudrillard's response to the attacks on the Twin Towers were akin to a mechanical form of critique that responds more or less the same way to any and all new events. What is even worse, though, than Baudrillard using critique in this way is teaching the next generation of critics to engage in critique in a similar fashion. "Would it not be rather terrible if we were still training young kids—yes, young recruits, young cadets—for wars that are no longer possible, fighting enemies long gone, conquering territories that no longer exist, leaving them ill-equipped in the face of threats we had not anticipated, for which we are so thoroughly unprepared?"

But the only revisionism here is that of Latour and Felski in trying imagine the humanities *without* critique. To scapegoat Baudrillard as exemplary of the limits of critique or to say that we need to use more "re-" prefixes in the humanities rather than "de-" prefixes is to resort to nothing more than a sophisticated effort to preserve neoliberalism. In short, if postcritique achieves anything, it is the negation of all efforts to bring about the demise of neoliberalism.

There is a great deal of unhappiness and disenchantment within academe today. The humanities are struggling to define their role in an academic world driven more by data and numbers than knowledge and ideas. The university itself has been the object of increasing levels of privatization, commodification, and corporatization. Many academics are scrambling to find solutions to these and other crises. But to blame "critique" for the problems facing the humanities in particular and the university in general shamelessly kowtows to the neoliberal agenda that is for the most part responsible for these crises.

Critique in its best form focuses on the ways in which domination manifests itself throughout our society, and empowers students with the tools to work to overcome it both symbolically and

49

institutionally. As a part of critical pedagogy, it asks for our educational systems to do more than just put information into the heads of students so that they can become "useful machines" for society. Rather, critical pedagogy seeks to produce citizens who are critical, self-reflective, and knowledgeable; who are responsible moral agents that see politics, education, and the economy as a continuum rather than separate spheres. Critical citizenship and democratic education provide democracy the backdrop it needs to be successful. In short, critique provides society with the hope that we can make the world better in terms of social and economic justice.

Postcritique aims to do away with critique and its social and political "baggage." Rather than educate students in what is needed for them to be a critical citizenry that espouses democratic values, it reverses the educational process by focusing on their own personal likes and dislikes. If the aim of critique is to learn to think, then the aim of postcritique is to learn how to *un*think. While I am not opposed to students developing "more sophisticated vocabularies for describing and justifying [their] feelings," this must not come at the expense of critique. But, unfortunately, it does for the postcritical crowd. Rather than educating students in critique, postcritics in America today, much like the academics in the German institutions of the nineteenth century, are caught up in "the ubiquitous encouragement of everyone's so-called 'individual personality.'" Nietzsche—one of Ricoeur's masters of suspicion—described this type of encouragement in his 1872 lectures on the future of educational institutions, "nothing but a mark of barbarity."

To see postcritique as a species of neoliberal thinking is to cast doubt on it—and to deny it any role in conversations about the future of the humanities. The future of theory depends on the continued viability of critique in the humanities. Likewise, the humanities without critique are nothing more than a service industry in the neoliberal academy. Our path out of the economic juggernaut of neoliberal academe requires critique and students who are taught how to build their dreams—educational and otherwise—on and with suspicious minds.

Contra the postcritics (and maybe Elvis too) we can and should go on together, particularly in the humanities, with suspicious minds.

6 | THE TOWN BOOK BUILDING

"The treasures of the world which books contain were opened to me at the right moment. The fundamental advantage of a library is that it gives nothing for nothing. Youths must acquire knowledge themselves."

—Andrew Carnegie, *Autobiography of Andrew Carnegie* (1920)

There was a fantastic gray stone building in my hometown that housed only books—not people.

One needed to climb a staircase and pass through two stone pillars to enter it.

Therein one discovered beautiful tiling, elegant crown molding, and other ornate features that only heightened the experience of seeking wisdom within its walls.

Its sturdy wooden bookcases held many treasures. One did not have to request them at the imposing front desk, but was rather allowed—if not encouraged—to leisurely browse the shelves.

I always managed to find through serendipity a stack of books that I excitedly brought back home for perusal.

However, for a young seeker of books, the difference between this building and our home could not have been starker.

Whereas the town book building was overflowing with amazing reading material, our home was not. In fact, there were no books in our home until an encyclopedia set purchased one volume at a time from the supermarket started to make its way into the living room.

But in this regard, our home was not very different from that of our neighbors.

None of their homes contained any books either. Moreover, even if there were a desire to purchase some, there were no bookstores—aside, that is, from the supermarket.

Thus, the gray stone building was for many of us the sole source of books in the area.

It was the only book building in our town—and as a child it felt as though it were the only book building in the world.

ॐ

In the first quarter of the twentieth-century, one of America's most powerful and wealthy philosophers, William Ernest Hocking, started the process of designing and constructing his own book building. It would be located just a few miles from William James's "summer" house in Chocorua, New Hampshire. To get to Hocking's building, one needed to travel to the small village of Madison, New Hampshire, and then ascend up a hill through a forest. There, among the white pine trees, one would find two Georgian-style stone buildings: one of them a large house; and the other the philosopher's book building.

Hocking was a master carpenter and once even a member of the American Federation of Labor, an early labor union. In 1906, the same year he started his professional philosophy career at the University of California, Berkeley, he also was a contract carpenter that helped to rebuild San Francisco after the great earthquake of April of that year. Ten years later, when he joined the army during World War One, he took up military engineering, where he went on to work with the U.S. Army civil engineers on the Western Front in 1917.

Then, in 1926, Hocking and his friend Fred Frost began to gather granite from the surrounding hills that would be used in the construction of the book building he would call "West Wind." The building technique he utilized, slipform masonry, was a new one. It involved combining metal bars, concrete, and rocks between a greased wooden frame. Fittingly, he learned it from a book—its title was *Building a Home: Save a Third*.

For most professional philosophers, let alone one that was the Alford Professor of Natural Religion, Moral Philosophy, and Civil Polity in the Department of Philosophy at Harvard University, this all might have seemed like a major departure. But for someone like Hocking, who dreamt of being an engineer or an architect before he was bitten by the philosophy bug in high school, and who had helped to rebuild a city that was razed by an earthquake and dealt with trench construction during a grisly war, the construction of a book building in the backwoods of New Hampshire was most likely a meaningful task and joyful labor.

Hocking was the first major American philosopher to build his own book building (unless, of course, we want to argue that Henry David Thoreau's cabin was the original "book building," which, though interesting, seems like a bit of a stretch in this context). It was home to an incredible collection of rare and important philosophy books—a collection that can provide some significant insights into the intellectual foundations of American philosophy.

Nevertheless, Hocking was also probably the last major American philosopher to take on the task of constructing a book building.

ea.

The book building in my hometown was not built by a famous philosopher.

And neither did it contain rare and important books, nor did its builders use slipform masonry or forage the countryside for the gray stones of its outer walls.

It was however funded by one of the greatest philanthropists in the world, and built in a town founded a few months after the start of the Civil War in what our "infamous" town's founder called "the wildest part of New Jersey." (Our town's founder was "infamous," first among many other reasons, because he shot a local newspaper editor in the back of the head just because he did not like statements the editor wrote about him in the newspaper—the editor seven months later fell into a coma and died from complications of the shot.)

In 1861, not yet thirty years old, Charles K. Landis founded my hometown on a virtually uninhabited tract of land of about forty-eight square miles. It would be the second town he founded in south Jersey but not the last. His intention was to make it "a vine country," thus he called it Vineland. But, though grapes would be grown in the town, they would not be used to produce wine because Landis deemed that the town would not allow taverns and alcohol consumption. Consequently, grape juice, not wine, was produced locally. Thomas B. Welch, who was an early settler in the town, invented in 1869 a process for making juice instead of wine from grapes grown in Vineland.

As a planned agricultural and industrial community, the town grew quickly. By 1865, it had 500 buildings, and at the time of Landis's death in 1900, there were even more buildings including large factories and plants. Nevertheless, at the turn of the century there was no book building in Vineland. Though the early settlers had established a library association, it did not succeed over the long term. All of this changed however on February 2, 1903 when the Carnegie Corporation of New York granted the town $12,000 to build a public library.

While not the first Carnegie library grant in New Jersey (East Orange received theirs on January 18, 1900) it was one of the earlier ones. In sum, the Carnegie Corporation over a period of 1900 to 1917 would provide over one million dollars in funding toward the construction of 36 book buildings around the Garden State. The one I frequented as a kid opened in 1906, and remained in use until a new book building was constructed in the 1970s. While the new building had none of the character and charisma (and smell) of the old Carnegie building, it had something much more utilitarian: it was significantly larger, and thus better able to serve a growing population.

Like many of the 2,509 book buildings that the Carnegie Corporation financed around the world between 1883 and 1929, including book buildings in Australia, Belgium, Canada, the Caribbean, Fiji, France, Ireland, Malaysia, Mauritius, New Zealand, Serbia, South Africa, and the United Kingdom, the old Carnegie building in Vineland is still in use. Today, however, it is a building for people (senior citizens)—not books.

In total, there were 1,689 book buildings around the United States in places like my hometown that were the direct consequence of the philanthropy of the Carnegie Corporation. If one also includes the 110 Carnegie supported book buildings on academic campuses, then the sum total expended in the U.S. alone on book buildings comes to nearly 46 million dollars. Adjusted for inflation (and just based on 1929 dollars rather than adjusting the donations by year for inflation back through 1883 and then calculating their sum, which would be even more), this comes to nearly *646 billion dollars* spent on book buildings in the first quarter of the twentieth century by the Carnegie Corporation.

Many of them are still in use as book buildings, others have been repurposed, and still others are no longer standing. But some too are just empty buildings—and a few are now even for sale.

In 2018, for example, the Carnegie book building in Elwood, Indiana was put up for sale. For a mere $95,000, you too can have your own book building just like William Ernest Hocking complete with two working fireplaces. Books not included.

❧

After Hocking died in 1966, his son Richard became the steward of his father's book building and its contents. Given that the building contained many philosophy books from the seventeenth and eighteenth century, and many other books with marginalia from previous owners like William James and Josiah Royce, one would think that finding a suitable new book building for them would not be difficult.

But it was.

Richard tried but failed on numerous occasions to donate the entire collection to Harvard University, the university where his father had taken Royce's position on the philosophy faculty. The problem was not that they did not want the Hocking collection. They did as it contained hundreds of valuable first editions of works of classic philosophy by Spinoza, Leibniz, Hobbes, Wolfe, Locke, Kant, Mill, and Hegel—in addition to works previously owned by some important American philosophers.

One of the books in Hocking's collection, for example, was a first edition of Hobbes's *Leviathan* (1651), and another was a first edition of Locke's (anonymously written) *Two Treatises of Government* (1690). A copy of the Hobbes volume alone was known to have been sold for $32,000, whereas Locke's *Two Treatises* went for even more, $41,000.

The problem was that Harvard did not want to be responsible for maintaining the *entire* contents of Hocking's book building. Rather, they wanted to cherry-pick the good stuff—and get rid of the rest. As a result, the contents of this book building more or less remained in tact long after his death—and then also after the death of his son in 2001.

Richard, who also became a professional philosopher, left his own collection of books on his father's property though not in his father's book building. Rather, they were stored in a barn in a field near the book building. Such was the reverence of the son toward his father's book building that he dared not defile its contents by adding his own books to it.

There are probably plenty a farm buildings around the country that serve as final resting places for academic book collections. I had the good fortune when I lived in the Northeast one summer to be gifted some books laid to rest in one such barn building. When the professor had a retired from a prestigious private university in the area, he left his book collection in his sister's barn. The sister, who knew I was a philosophy student, invited me over one day to go through them and take what I wanted.

No first edition Hobbes, but some Freud that I still treasure.

ૐ

The fate of the book collections of academics is generally not a pretty one.

Years of meticulously acquired books in support of narrow research interests often just end up being scoured and scavenged by colleagues and students in an afternoon. The remaining titles end up in boxes set out in the hallway or are donated to charity. While some of these collections may be valuable to book dealers and collectors, because academics tend to be hard on their books—they underline sentences, write in the margins, break the bindings, spill coffee on them, and even tear out pages—most are often only fit for recycling by other academics. Who, then, when their need for them is over, pass them along to other academics. Such is the life cycle of old academic books, even those by philosophical masters such as Hobbes, Hegel, and Hocking.

Hocking's book building was by all accounts a shrine to a body of American philosophical masters who participated in this academico-biblio life cycle. It contained a lot of books marked up and formerly owned by some of the famous philosophers who were his teachers and friends. As Hocking was one of the last students who studied philosophy at Harvard with the "Big Four"—William James, Josiah Royce, George Herbert Palmer, and George Santayana—many of the books in his collection were previously owned by them.

For example, he owned a copy of Kant's *Kritik der Reinen Vernunft* heavily annotated by William James. But he also had acquired books that they had acquired. For example, he owned a complete leather-bound set of the first run (1867 to 1893) of *The Journal of Speculative Philosophy*. Judging by the signature in the first volume of the set, it was at one time owned by "Charles S. Peirce," who also happened to publish some of his best work in the journal during this time period. How it got into Hocking's hands is anyone's guess but it was probably a legacy acquisition from one of his former teachers or colleagues.

The presence of hundreds of annotated tomes in Hocking's book building was recently brought to national attention by a young philosophy professor from New England. John Kaag's excellent book, *American Philosophy: A Love Story* (2016), provides many interesting details and stories about these and other books he found in West Wind. Centered around his chance visit in 2008 to Hocking's book building, and subsequent multi-year exploration of its contents, *American Philosophy* tells the story of how he "saved" these books which had come to be in bad shape due to years of neglect.

In fact, the year before Kaag discovered the book collection, one of Hocking's relatives was in such despair about their condition, he decided to steal some of them. "High on heroin," he packed up 400 rare books from West Wind and shipped them to his home in Berkeley, California. The FBI, however, recovered most of them. When caught, the thief claimed he stole them just to "protect them" and that he "had no plans to sell [them] for money."

Kaag though was not the first philosopher to know about and recognize the importance of the Hocking collection. Douglas Anderson, for example, who is also a philosophy professor, had for years tried to convince his friend, Richard Hocking, to "save" the books. Kaag was, however, the first to actually get them out of this abandoned book building and into the hands of people who would appreciate them—get them out, that is, without stealing them.

Through his efforts, some were donated to the university archives where he works. Others, like the annotated volumes, are now in the process of being digitally scanned so that the marginalia of folks likes James can be studied by scholars.

All told, even after a half of century sitting abandoned and unused in the woods, the books—for better or worse—somehow managed to avoid the scouring and scavenging of colleagues and students that is usual fate of academic books.

ಸ

57

But the lesson of this particular book building is about much more than just the fate of its contents.

Here was a professor who was at the center of the American philosophical world for most of his life. He knew and corresponded with just about every major thinker in his many areas of interest including world religion, ethics, metaphysics, and political philosophy. He wrote letters to an astounding 7,236 individuals including many American presidents. Still, we learn from Kaag that in the 1980s, Hocking's son Richard, had to pay "Harvard no small amount of money" to house his correspondence. And, as we've already determined, Harvard did not want his books. Or, perhaps, given the fate of his letters, Hocking's family did not have enough money to pay Harvard to house his books as well.

This now brings us full circle to a modest proposal regarding collections like Hocking's: why not utilize some of those abandoned but still standing Carnegie book buildings to house collections like the one left behind by Hocking?

Rather than relegating these incredible collections to the dark archives of a university or allowing them to dissipate into the random hands of colleagues and students (and thieves), put them to public use and display in the buildings that Andrew Carnegie built in the United States to spread knowledge.

Carnegie did not build these book buildings for the masses that would choose not to benefit from them. But rather, he built them for the much smaller slice of the public that would choose to benefit from them. He thought the value to this smaller group of the community outweighed the lack of benefit they brought to the larger masses.

There were 1,406 towns in the United States where book buildings were constructed with Carnegie funds. While the vast majority were in the Midwest, Carnegie book buildings were built in 46 states.

Imagine some of them coming back to life and use as shrines for the book collections and archives of American scholars who spent their life in the pursuit of knowledge.

Now imagine people, young and old, entering these shrines and being inspired to read and think about democratic values and critical citizenship.

Throw a digital book scanner into each of these book buildings for those worried about the physical fate of these collections, and you have a perfect twenty-first century spin on nineteenth-century public book culture.

This new use of old town book buildings would be a further fulfillment of Carnegie's philanthropic vision of public education— and a great service to the advancement of knowledge in America.

7 | DARK SHADOWS

"This man can either do you a great deal of good—or a great deal of harm. He must be taken in small doses. Had I discovered Schopenhauer at twenty-one, I would either have lived a very beautiful and complete life by thirty—or been dead. That I should believe you'll take the good and leave the bad from these complexities almost proves how very dear you are to me."

—Ted 4/19/35

How responsible are we for the potentially life-altering consequences of the books that we share with others for reading? Or does our obligation end after we place the book in their hands?

On April 19, 1935, at the height of the Great Depression, a man named Ted gave his young acquaintance a beautiful hardbound edition of the writings of Arthur Schopenhauer. He also warned this person of the potential consequences of reading Western philosophy's arch-pessimist.

Reading Schopenhauer "can either do you a great deal of good—or a great deal of harm" says Ted in his inscription. Interestingly, the name of the person to whom the book is inscribed is literally cut out from the page though the rest of the inscription remains.

What happened to this person? Were they dead by thirty or did they lead a "very beautiful and complete life"? And what role did reading Schopenhauer play in all of this? The inscription sets a portentious tone to reading a philosopher who already is notorious for casting a dark shadow over the world.

The book was published by the Tudor Publishing Company of New York in 1933. Its editor, James Gibson Hume, similarly warns the reader about Schopenhauer stating that he stands "alone" among philosophers and "cannot be classified." Hume continues,

59

Schopenhauer explicitly announces that he is in open revolt against every so-called orthodox position. His work is throughout a protest. He naturally attracts to him every one who is dissatisfied . . . .

But so too does Friedrich Nietzsche. Together, these two philosophers form a perfect set of pessimistic bookends. All the better that the youthful Nietzsche idolized Schopenhauer only to distance himself later in life from the "cadaverous perfume" of his philosophy. For Nietzsche, Schopenhauer's philosophy is a life-denying approach to the world, whereas, in contrast, he sees his own approach as "life-affirming."

Be that as it may, not everyone is convinced of the need for pessimism. "Pessimism," writes Eugene Thacker in *Cosmic Pessimism* (2015), "is the philosophical form of disenchantment." It is also "the lowest form of philosophy, frequently disparaged and dismissed, merely the symptom of a bad attitude." "No one ever needs pessimism," continues Thacker, "in the way that one needs optimism to inspire one to great heights and to pick oneself up, in the way one needs constructive criticism, advice and feedback, inspirational books or a pat on the back."

But in a society where individuals are systemically subject to domination, exploitation, and fear, and where they do not have agency or enjoy democratic values, pessimism can give individual disenchantment with the world a philosophical outlet. Still, it needs to be tempered lest it lead to complete nihilism and despair.

જ.

The first of two editions of Schopenhauer's *The World as Will and Idea* was published in 1819 when he was thirty years old. The following year, Schopenhauer lectured at the University of Berlin but did not attract much of a following, in part because his lectures were held at the same hour that Hegel lectured.

Schopenhauer argues in this book that in life suffering is fundamental, universal, and unavoidable. Moreover, for him, real satisfaction in life is not obtainable. "The truth is," claims Schopenhauer, "we ought to be wretched, and we are so."

In contradistinction to the "palpably sophistical proofs of Leibniz that this is the best of all possible worlds," comments

Schopenhauer, "we may honestly oppose the proof that it is the worst of all possible worlds." His "proof" is as follows:

> Now this world is so arranged as to be able to maintain itself with great difficulty; but if it were a little worse, it could not maintain itself. Consequently a worse world, since it could not continue to exist, is absolutely impossible: this world is the worst of all possible worlds.

Schopenhauer confirms his pessimism by claiming that it can be found throughout the philosophical tradition dating back to the ancient Greeks. In fact, if he "were to give what has been said by great men of all ages in this anti-optimistic spirit, there would be no end to the quotations, for almost every one of them has expressed in strong language his knowledge of the misery of this world."

For Schopenhauer, evidence that the Greeks were "deeply affected by the wretchedness of existence" can be shown, for example, by "the invention of tragedy" and the fact that the Thracians had the "custom of welcoming the new-born child with lamentations, and recounting all the evils which now lie before it; and, on the other hand, burying the dead with mirth and jesting, because they are no longer exposed to so many and great sufferings." Even Socrates in Plato's *Apology*, reports Schopenhauer, says that "death, even if it deprives us of consciousness for ever, would be a wonderful gain, for a deep, dreamless sleep every day is to be preferred even to the happiest life."

"Everything in life shows that early happiness is destined to be frustrated or recognized as an illusion," writes Schopenhauer. "Happiness accordingly always lies in the future, or else in the past, and the present may be compared to a small dark cloud which the wind drives over the sunny plain: before and behind it all is bright, only it itself always casts a shadow."

61

ॐ

As educators, we might now ask how the dark shadows of pessimism extend as well into our field. Interestingly, though both Schopenhauer and Nietzsche were concerned about and wrote on the future of education, their pessimism regarding it went in different directions.

In the case of Schopenhauer, education offers us the opportunity to escape from the slavery of the will. His refined Kantianism combined the latter's phenomenal world of appearances and representations with a reformulated noumenal world. Whereas for Kant, the noumenon, the thing-in-itself, can never be known to us, for Schopenhauer, this noumenal world was transformed into a central all-embracing notion of the "will." For him, "the whole [physical] body is nothing but objectified will, i.e., will become idea."

Moreover, through the world of representation or idea, the will acquires knowledge of its own willing. Writes Schopenhauer, "the word *will*, which like a magic spell, discloses to us the inmost being of everything in nature, is by no means an unknown quantity, something arrived at only by inference, but is fully and immediately comprehended, and is so familiar to us that we know and understand what will is far better than anything else whatever." Nevertheless, while the will "always knows what it wills now and here, [it] never [knows] what it wills in general." Consequently, the will in itself is merely blind, irrational striving—"a constant striving without end and without rest" and with "an unquenchable thirst."

For Schopenhauer, this irrational striving of the will and the fact that for him the satisfaction of the will is a contradiction in terms makes his pessimism totalizing. For him, "life swings like a pendulum backwards and forwards between pain and ennui." When the will "lacks objects of desire, because it is at once deprived of them by a too easy satisfaction, a terrible void and ennui comes over it"; but when the will is in the throws of its unquenchable thirsts, "the nature of brutes and man is subject to pain originally and through its very being." In short, *life is suffering*.

Still, despite Schopenhauer's bleak account of the life of humans and the world, he is nonetheless concerned that through education we acquire unprejudiced knowledge of the world. "*To acquire a knowledge of the world* might be defined as the aim of all education," writes Schopenhauer. The "artificial method" of education "is to hear what other people say, to learn and to read, and so to get your head crammed full of general ideas before you have any sort of extended acquaintance with the world as it is, and as you may see it for yourself." While it is hoped that the "general ideas" that are "crammed" into your head are verified by particular observation, "until that time arrives, you apply your general ideas wrongly, you judge men and things from a wrong standpoint, you see them in a wrong light, and treat them in a wrong way." Thus, for Schopenhauer, the artificial method of education "perverts the mind."

Nevertheless, Schopenhauer held out the hope that formal education could at least attempt to avoid perverting the mind by endeavoring to always "let particular observations precede general ideas and not *vice versa* as is usually and unfortunately the case." While book knowledge has its place, it is limited especially with young learners. "Instead, therefore, of hastening to place *books*, and books alone, in [children's] hands, let them be made acquainted, step by step, with *things*—with the actual circumstances of human life."

The path of education without prejudice is hard enough for Schopenhauer, "but the difficulty is doubled by *novels*, which represent a state of things in life and the world, such as, in fact, does not exist." The "false view of things" arrived at through reading novels "exercises a baneful influence on [the young person's] whole life." Though there are a few exceptions to this rule such as Walter Scott's novels, Schopenhauer contends that Cervantes's novel *Don Quixote* is "a satirical exhibition of the error to which [he is] referring."

Yet, in spite of his warnings about the dangers of reading novels and emphasis on acquiring knowledge of the state of things in life and the world, Schopenhauer maintains that the arts can provide a *reprieve* from the suffering of the world. In particular, he believes that one of the ways of escaping from the slavery of the will is through aesthetics. This is particularly true in the case of music, which Schopenhauer regards as "the most powerful of all the arts." For him, "music acts directly upon the will, i.e., the feelings, passions, and emotions of the hearer, so that it quickly raises them or changes them."

Musical affect is accomplished because music, "unlike all the other arts, does not express the Ideas, or grades of objectification of the will, but directly the *will itself*." Thus, according to his metaphysics of music, it "exalts our minds," elevating them above the suffering of the world and removing the intellect from the servitude of the will. Still, Schopenhauer wants to be clear that though the affect of music on the will "seems to us to speak of other and better worlds than ours [which is 'the worst of all possible worlds'], yet really it only flatters the will to live, because it exhibits to it its nature, deludes it with the images of

63

its success, and at the end expresses its satisfaction and contentment." It stands to reason, therefore, that because music flatters and deludes the will to live, it is probably best kept out of the hands of the young because the aim of their education is to learn the world as it is—not as it might be.

In contrast to Schopenhauer, who finds in education the search for knowledge of the world through empirical observation, Nietzsche seems to believe that if we just rely upon empirical observation of the human animal, the only thing we will find are conflicting ways of life and values. Moreover, Nietzsche contends that "[t]o divide the world into a 'real' and an 'apparent' world, whether in the manner of Christianity or in the manner of Kant (which is, after all, that of a *cunning* Christian—) is only a suggestion of *décadence*—a symptom of a *declining* life)."

For Nietzsche, "one of the highest tasks of formal education" is to "inculcate serious and unrelenting critical habits." However, German formal education, that is, both its gymnasiums, which prepare students for the university, and the universities themselves, are in Nietzsche's opinion failing in this regard. Rather than educating students in critique, German institutions are caught up—as noted earlier—in "the ubiquitous encouragement of everyone's so-called 'individual personality,'" which Nietzsche considers "nothing but a mark of barbarity."

Formal education in Germany is failing, argues Nietzsche in his 1872 lectures on the future of German educational institutions, because of both its "drive for the greatest possible *expansion* and *dissemination* of education" and its "drive for the *narrowing* and *weakening* of education." The first drive extends it too widely and pushes it upon those who may not need or want it; the second makes it subject to the needs of the state and thereby requires it to relinquish its independence. "It is in journalism that the two tendencies converge: education's expansion and its narrowing," which "reduces scholars to being mere slaves of academic disciplines." "The daily newspaper has effectively replaced education, and anyone who still lays claim to culture or education, even a scholar, typically relies on a sticky layer of journalism—a substance as sturdy and permanent as the paper it's printed on—to grout the gaps between every form of life, every social position, every art, every science, every field." "The newspaper," concludes Nietzsche, "epitomizes the goal of today's educational system, just as the journalist, servant of the present moment, has taken the place of the genius, our salvation, from the moment and leader for the ages."

The educational expansion that Nietzsche refers to is part of the "national-economic doctrines" that see education only as a training ground for state service. A push then is made by the state for *rapid education, so that you can start earning money quickly, and at the same time a thorough education so that you can earn lots of money.*" "Culture," within this rapid education model, "is tolerated only insofar as it serves the cause of earning money." In direct opposition to Schopenhauer, Nietzsche concludes, "humanity has a necessary claim to earthly happiness and that is why education is necessary— but that is only reason why!"

While Nietzsche is not opposed to the acquiring wealth, he is opposed to *Bildung* that thwarts the process of self-education that aims to produce a "true culture" within oneself. The German word for "education," *Bildung*, though has other meanings including enlightenment, culture, inner development, sculpting, and shaping. As Paul Reitter and Chad Wellmon, editors of Nietzsche's 1872 lectures (which they intriguingly entitle *Anti-Education* [2016]) note, "*Bildung* is not simply education but the process, achieved through education, of forming the most desirable self; it is also the ideal endpoint of that process: attaining or undergoing *Bildung* means acquiring and entering true culture." In Nietzsche's opinion, the German educational system thwarts self-cultivation when it "reduces scholars to being mere slaves of academic disciplines"—something that makes "it a matter of chance, and increasingly unlikely, for any scholar to turn out truly *educated*." In fact, in Germany "[t]here is a need for educators *who are themselves educated.*"

To reverse this decline in German education, Nietzsche says that there must be a greater emphasis placed on classical education (Greek and Roman) and learning the German language. But this comes at a cost: namely, the democratization of education. Perhaps the real problem with education's expansion and its narrowing for Nietzsche is its relation to "privilege": "That 'higher education' is no longer a privilege—the democratism of 'culture' made 'universal' and *common.*" As such, Nietzsche's educational pessimism is fundamentally flawed by contemporary standards.

While we can agree with claims like "Learning to *think*: our schools no longer have any idea what this means" and sympathize with his worries about "expansion and narrowing" as well as the relative failures of education to instill "unrelenting critical habits," Nietzsche's recommendations for a return to educational privilege and emphasis on "high" culture (Greek and Roman) are not timely today. At the same time, his belief "[t]he essential thing has gone out of the entire system of higher education in Germany: the *end*, as well as the *means* to the end" holds as well for our current educational situation.

Neoliberal academe has corrupted both the *means* and *ends* of education. For Nietzsche, "[t]hat education, *culture*, itself is the end . . . has been forgotten" is a good place to start educational pessimism; however, to end it with a call for a return to educational privilege is not a viable solution. By comparison, Schopenhauer, who leaves his pessimism about the world in tact while retaining the lofty goal of *acquiring a knowledge of the world* as the aim of all education" seems preferable to Nietzsche's self-cultivation.

٭

Nietzsche and Schopenhauer are classic resources for those dissatisfied with philosophical orthodoxies and the status quo. Consequently, they can be a philosophical outlet not only for individuals—young and old—who are dissatisfied with life in general, but also academics who are continually pessimistic about academe's prospects and unhappy with academic life. Both were university professors, and both were concerned about the future of education though their pessimism regarding it differed significantly. A dose of the dark shadows of pessimism for a world that appears everywhere to be going wrong does not sound like something for which we need to warn off readers today—especially if it encourages protest and revolt among the dissatisfied.

8 | THE SELF-PUBLISHING REVOLUTION

Each year more books are being published worldwide than the previous year. In the U.K. alone, it was recently estimated that in just one year 184,000 new titles were published. And even more books were produced the same year in China and the United States. It is debatable though whether this is good news.

Jonny Geller, a literary agent at the New York entertainment agency, Curtis Brown, Ltd., said that growth like this is "either a sign of cultural vitality or publishing suicide." "Of course," he continues, "it is utter madness to publish so many books when the average person reads between one and five books a year, but would you prefer 184,000 new brands of shoes or pointless luxury items?" "In fact," concludes Geller, "don't answer that."

But, for others, more books published annually is a positive thing. "For the vibrancy of culture," comments Roland Philipps, managing director of the British publisher John Murray, "books are essential, and if publishers are taking on more they must believe that voices are deserving to be heard, even if not all those voices make an impact with the consumer."

Still—hundreds of thousands of new brands of shoes aside— it is difficult to form a concrete image of the current rate of book production growth. The physicist Steven Hawking tried though to do this by speculating how fast one would have to travel to keep up with annual book production. "If you stacked the new books being published next to each other," wrote the physicist in *Brief Answers to the Big Questions* (2018), "at the present rate of production you would have to move at ninety miles an hour just to keep up with the end of the line." But unlike Philipps, for Hawking this rapid rate of growth is not a good thing. "If the exponential growth continued," said Hawking, "there would be ten papers a second in my kind of theoretical physics, and no time to read them."

Moreover, this type of complaint about publishing growth is not just limited to new work in physics. The most recent numbers on just fiction produced annually in the U.S. set it at around 50,000 new titles per year. Given that there are 525,600 minutes in a year, if you did nothing else all year but read these new titles, you would only have on average about 10½ minutes to peruse each one. Hawking of course was projecting into the future with his calculation—and not focusing on present output. Given that there are 31,557,600 seconds in a year, and Hawking says that based on the current rate of growth he would need to read 10 papers a second, his projection for just new articles in theoretical physics is 315.5 billion per year.

If this were not dystopian enough, Hawking also adds that in the year 2600 (or about 250 years after the time period of *Star Trek*) all "new artistic and scientific work will come in electronic forms rather than physical books and papers." Thus, according to one of the greatest minds of our time, in about six hundred years new books and articles will not only come out exclusively in electronic form, but these new works will be so voluminous that it will be impossible for humans to keep up with new research and creative work in their area of interest.

Even if we generally sympathize with those who complain that the amount of new fiction currently produced in the U.S. makes it impossible to keep up with it as a scholar or writer of contemporary American fiction, in about six hundred years the present output of new fiction will seem manageable in terms of overall comprehension in comparison to the billions of works of new fiction produced annually in a not so distant future. But there is another way to look at the exponential growth in publishing that embraces its voluminous future. Its source is not a physicist or contemporary scholar of American literature. Or even a publisher or literary agent, but an organization dedicated to supporting the establishment of a better world: the United Nations.

☙

Since 1951, the United Nations (UN) has monitored both the number and type of books published per country per year. The third issue of the UN *Statistical Yearbook*, prepared by the Statistical Office of the United Nations, Department of Economic Affairs, unceremoniously announced this as follows: "The other new tables introduced in the present *Statistical Yearbook* cover production of canned fish, numbers of wireless receiving sets (radios) in use, production of books and production of long (feature) films."

Book production information in 1951 was provided for 16 countries from Africa, North America, South America, Asia, Europe, and Oceania.[1] The subject areas covered in the first UN book production report were Generalities, Philosophy, Religion, Social Sciences, Philology, Pure Sciences, Applied Sciences, Arts, Literature, Geography/History, and Unspecified. The UN continued to provide data on book production across the world for the next fifty years.

The 2001 *Statistical Yearbook* (forty-eighth issue), which contained data available as of 15 December 2003, would be the last *Statistical Yearbook* to include book production data. The subject areas covered in the last report were Generalities, Philosophy/Psychology, Religion/Theology, Social Sciences, Philology (which is now explained as the "History of Literature and Literary Criticism"), Pure Sciences, Applied Sciences, Arts and Recreation, Literature, and Geography/History. Book production information in this report was provided for 105 countries from Africa, North America, South America, Asia, Europe, and Oceania.

For the next three years, the UN *Yearbook* listed book production in the table of contents though with the proviso that it was only to "identify tables present in previous issues of the *Statistical Yearbook* but not contained in the present issue." Nevertheless, it also said, "These tables will be updated in future issues of the *Yearbook* when new data become available." This practice would continue in the 2003 and 2004 *Statistical Yearbooks* until finally in the 2005 *Statistical Yearbook*, which included data available as of June 2008, there was no mention of book production in the "Culture and Communication" section where it had usually been listed.

However, with the disappearance of "Book Production" data came the introduction of "Internet Users" data in the 1998 *Statistical Yearbook*, which listed data available as of 30 November 2000. This first listing was by country and covered the period 1990 through 1999. The most recent listing, in the 2018 *Statistical Yearbook* provides internet usage figures for 227 countries and areas, covering the years 2000, 2005, 2010, 2013, 2014, and 2016.

In short, the UN considered book production an important index of the standard of living and education in a country, and an important indicator of a country's cultural vitality and national self-awareness until either 15 December 2003, the last year book production data was *provided* for the 2001 *Statistical Yearbook* (forty-eighth issue) or March 2007, the last year book production data was *promised* for the 2004 *Statistical Yearbook* (fifty-first issue). The latter date though is preferable given that the Kindle Reader was introduced a few months later, on November 19, 2007, officially launching the era of digital book euphoria.

In the hands of the United Nations, book production data was less a measure of one person or scholar's ability to master a growing field of creativity or scholarship, than the measure of a nation's relative *biopolitical* health. The use of the term biopolitics here is a reference to Michel Foucault's introduction of the concept in his lectures at the Collège de France in the mid-1970s, where he discusses "forecasts, statistical estimates, and overall measures" similar to the ones utilized by the United Nations in their *Statistical Yearbooks*. Relatively speaking, by the UN's measuring stick—at least for a period of 50 years—countries that produced more books annually either per capita or per nation were healthier than nations that produced less. This is a very different way to look at book production than the narcissistic scholarly window that only sees the totality of book production through the lens of one person, rather than from the position of the country or community who are producing the new creative and scholarly works.

Yet since the UN stopped monitoring worldwide book publication data (and replaced it with "Internet Users"), it has been difficult to determine both book production by country and overall production worldwide. Even the International Publishers Association (IPA), which was established in 1896 and "aims at mapping international book publishing markets," confesses that

> Mapping and analyzing these developments involves confronting several layers of complexities, notably a lack of standard definitions even for the most generic parameters, such as what kind of publishing should be included and which sectors can be excluded (e.g. newspapers, magazines, or business and wire services). Furthermore, even the most basic statistical references are available for only a very limited number of countries.

These constraints limited their reporting to only forty countries. Sadly enough, it is an evolving entry from Wikipedia that is left to fill in the gap resulting from both the abandonment of UN monitoring of book production worldwide and the limitations of IPA reporting. This Wikipedia entry, "Books Published per Country per Year," is based on the 105 countries formerly monitored by the UN. It "updates" UN data where possible though there are many gaps in the entry. Nevertheless, it sets the current number of books published worldwide at 2.2 million.

Thus, based on this updated UN data and IPA reporting, the top four book producing countries are China (440,000 new titles per year), the United States (304,912), the United Kingdom (184,000), and Russia (101,981). Of the 123 countries listed in the Wikipedia entry, these are the only ones with over 100,000 new titles produced per year. Moreover, 113 of the 123 countries listed produced less than 50,000 new books per year; 86 out of the 123 produced less than 10,000 new books per year; 77 out of 123 produced less than 5,000; 65 out of 123 produced less than 2,000; and 56 out of 123 countries listed produced fewer than 1,000 new titles per year.

Again, because book production numbers per country are notoriously difficult to obtain particularly without the aid of a massive international organization such as the UN regularly collecting them, the dates used in the updated UN entry range from the more recent to the dated 1990 data from Monaco (41 books), Namibia (106 books), Tanzania (172 books), and Afghanistan (2,795 books). Even in the case of the United States, the most current information available to the public dates back to a report from Bowker that lists actual 2012 numbers and projected 2013 numbers by subject area. The 2013 number used by the updated UN data entry and the IPA report for the United States are the *projected* 2013 numbers of traditionally published titles, that is, 304,912. The most recent actual number Bowker reports is 309,957 new titles published in 2012, which is actually slightly more titles than they projected for the following year.

However, what the updated UN entry and the IPA report do not include are the non-traditional/unclassified numbers for either 2012 or 2013. In the case of the Bowker report, where both drew their data, non-traditional/unclassified numbers "consist of reprints

71

(often public domain), other titles printed on-demand, and wiki-based material." It also includes "records received too late to receive subject classification and/or ISBNs that were not classifiable."

If both of these sources for book production in the U.S. had used these "non-traditional/unclassified "numbers, then in 2012 the U.S. *alone* would have produced more books than the total estimated amount produced by every other country in the world. Why? Because the other number on the Bowker report is over 2 million non-traditional/unclassified titles produced in the U.S. in 2012 in addition to the 309,957 traditionally published titles. In short, the actual total of books produced in the United States in 2012 was 2.3 million titles. The projected number for the following year was 1.4 million titles. Either way, inclusion of these total publishing numbers would dwarf the production numbers of every other country in the world.

One can assess these numbers either by total books produced *or* per capita. By the former measure, the top five countries in order of rank are China, the United States, the United Kingdom, Russia, and India (90,000 new titles in 2013). However, if we look at book production by per capita, then the ranking changes radically with the United Kingdom (2,875 titles per million inhabitants [TPM]), Taiwan (1,831 TPM), Slovenia (1,831 TPM), Spain (1,626 TPM), and Georgia (1,547 TPM) topping out the list. According to this per capita ranking, which was done by the International Publishing Association, the remainder of the top 10 are the Czech Republic (1,509 TPM), Norway (1,275 TPM), Australia (1,176), Germany (1,156 TPM), and France (1,008 TPM) with the United States (989 TPM) coming in twelfth just after Italy (1,002 TPM).

The other factor is of course Gross Domestic Product per capita (GDPpC), which is determined by dividing the countries' GDP by its population. Here are the GDPpC figures for the top twelve per capita book producing countries: United Kingdom (36.2), Taiwan (41.5), Slovenia (27.9), Spain (32.1), Georgia (7.1), Czech Republic (27.3), Norway (65.4), Australia (43.5), Germany (43.3), France (36.9), Italy (34.3), and the United States (53.1).

Let's now take the TPM and divide it by GDPpC, and call this figure "Book Production Value." According to Book Production Value (BPV), among the top twelve TPM countries, the United States (18.6 BPV) and Slovenia (65.6 BPV) do not change in terms of ranking. And the United Kingdom (79.4 BPV), Australia (27.0 BPV), Spain (50.6 BPV) and Germany (26.7 BPV), each move down one ranking; and Taiwan (44.1 BPV) and Norway (19.5) both decrease by four places. However, the Czech Republic (55.3 BPV) increases by two places, France (27.3 BPV) and Italy (29.2) by three places, and finally, Georgia, with an incredible 217.0 BPV, increases by four places to become the highest ranked country in terms of Book Production Value.

But something even more interesting happens if we go back to the "non-traditional/unclassified" numbers that *both* the updated UN entry *and* the International Publishing Association report did not account for in their U.S. book production figures. If one were to take these figures into account in determining book production in the U.S. then not only would its overall national book production ranking change as noted earlier (the U.S. would be by far the largest producer of books of any country in the world), but its TPM and BPV rankings would change as well. Let's now go back to those figures and recalculate both the United States TPM and BPV rankings.

In 2013, Bowker projected that there would be 304,912 traditionally published books in the United States, and 1,108,183 non-traditionally published titles for a total of 1,413,095 books published. If we use the combined total (1,413,095 titles) as opposed to just the traditionally published title projections (304,912), then the U.S. "titles per million" goes from a 959 TPM to 4,444 TPM, which far outpaces the United Kingdom's 2,875 titles per million inhabitants.

We can now take this new 4,444 U.S. TPM and recalculate its Book Production Value, which now goes from a 18.6 BPV to a 83.7 BPV, second only Georgia's phenomenal 217.9 BPV. But we must remember that the numbers used by both the updated UN entry and the International Publishing Association were *projected* numbers for 2013. If they used the most recent *actual* numbers available, both the United States TPM and BPV would be even higher.

In 2012, Bowker set traditionally published books at 309,957 and non-traditionally published books at 2,042,840, for a total of 2,352,797 books published. Unlike the 2013 numbers used by both the updated UN entry and the International Publishing Association, these were not projected figures but rather actual ones. If we use the combined 2012 total (2,352,797 titles) as opposed to just the traditionally published title projections (304,912), then U.S. "titles

73

per million" goes from 959 TPM to 7,400 TPM, which far outpaces *both* the United Kingdom's 2,875 titles per million inhabitants and the recalibrated 2013 U.S. 4,444 TPM based on projected figures.

In addition, if we now take this 7,400 TPM and recalculate U.S. Book Production Value, it goes from a 18.6 BPV (based on projected 2013 traditional publishing figures) to a 83.7 BPV (based on combined projected 2013 traditional *and* non-traditional publishing figures—second only Georgia's phenomenal 217.9 BPV) to a 139.4 BPV, which is still second to Georgia's BPV but still even further ahead of the United Kingdom's third place 79.4 BPV.

કૈ

So what does this all mean for both the U.S. and international publishing world? For one thing, given that so much publishing in the United States is non-traditional, it seems only appropriate to include it in calculations of its relative position to publishing across the world. Arguably both the updated UN entry and the International Publishing Association reporting should take these numbers into consideration when estimating book production across the globe. But even though some numbers from Bowker with respect to "traditional publishing" versus "non-traditional publishing" have been provided, what exactly is meant by this distinction?

The International Association of Professional Writers and Editors (IAPWE) is good place to start. According to the IAPWE, "traditional publishers" are "companies that actually invest their money and resources (like marketing and printing) into the promise that books will sell." Moreover, traditional publishers "purchase [the] rights to manuscripts and pay royalties to authors, often offering advances prior to publishing."

Non-traditional publishers, however, do not generally "invest their money and resources" into things like the promotion, editing, and printing of the books they publish. Nor do they "purchase [the] rights to [the] manuscripts" they are publishing or "pay royalties" or offer "advances" to the authors whose work they are publishing. Generally speaking, non-traditional publishing falls into two categories though the boundaries between them are becoming less and less clear.

On the one hand, there is "true self-publishing," which the IAPWE says involves "companies like Lulu and BookBaby [which] provide services including cover design, editing, and print-on-demand publishing." According to the IAPWE, self-publishers make the author "responsible for registering the copyright and ISBN, production management, and marketing"—though a quick trip to the internet reveals that many self-publishing companies will do all of these things for you, and more, including "ghostwriting" your book, all for a price that is often listed on their website.

On the other hand, the IAPWE juxtaposes "true self-publishing" to "vanity publishing," which is also termed "subsidy publishing." Vanity publishing "differs from self-publishing in that the author assumes all the risk and pays the publisher." According to the IAPWE,

> This is counterproductive to authors trying to make money on their books. While vanity presses do offer services like cover design and editing, there is a major catch. Once a manuscript is published by a subsidy, it becomes their property, right down to the ISBN number. The author forfeits all rights to the book once it appears in the publisher's catalog.

While the distinctions made by the IAPWE are appreciated, especially if you are an author who wants to maximize the financial return on your self-publishing investment, from the perspective of the interests of reportage on books published per country, these issues should be moot. Who paid for the publication of the book and who profits from its publication should not be a factor in determining the total book production of a country, the number of titles it produces per capita, and its Book Production Value.

Furthermore, the case for including "non-traditional" publications in national considerations of book production became even stronger this year. Why? Because it was widely reported last fall that the number of self-published books in the United States surpassed the one million mark for the first time in publishing history. According to Bowker, in 2017 there were 1,009,188 ISBN numbers assigned to self-published books. The previous year, the number was 786,935. This was a one-year increase of 28 percent. In fact, since 2012, when the number of self-published books was

394,132 titles, the number of self-published books has not only increased annually, but over just this six-year period it has risen 156 percent. Given that the number of traditionally published books has remained relatively consistent during this same six-year period, or, alternately, has not come anywhere close to 156% growth, it seems fair and safe to say that *self-publishing is the major book production force in the United States*. Even though these self-published books might not appear from the industry perspective equivalent to "traditionally published" ones, book publishing in the U.S. has been revolutionized in the new millennium.

What was once an outsider in the publishing world is now a revolution that has turned book publishing over to a mass American audience. To not count self-published books toward the total book production of a country misrepresents its intellectual and creative life. The rapid increase in number of titles produced per capita in the U.S. and its Book Production Value should be a point of pride among Americans.

The United Nations had it right. Book production *is* an important index of the standard of living and education in a country, and an important indicator of the country's self-awareness. And, at least by this measure, our country is in good health compared to the rest of the world. Is it too much of a reach to regard the self-publishing revolution as the second American revolution? If this revolt is described as freedom from the tyranny of traditional publishing, then the answer should be obvious.

9 | TUMBLEWEED CONNECTIONS

The Annual Meeting of the Modern Languages Association of America is one of the high points of the academic year. Scholars from English, comparative literature, and foreign language departments from across the United States convene after the winter holidays for four days of scholarly presentations, book exhibitions, and—for the fortunate few— job interviews. This event is both a barometer of the relative health of one of the largest branches of the humanities as well as one of the few opportunities we have to see our profession and its participants in action.

Hundreds of sessions are organized on the wide-ranging themes and issues that represent the current interests and needs of the members of the MLA. To get a sense of the range, this past fall,[2] the first two sessions were "Fund-Raising 101: How to Raise Money for Your Programs and Events" (Session 001) and "DH Curious? Digital Humanities Tools and Technologies for Students, Emerging Scholars, Faculty Members, Librarians, and Administrators" (Session 002), and the last two sessions were devoted to "Marxism and the Future of Higher Education" (Session 746) and "Critical Race Theory and New Directions for Victorian Studies" (Session 747).

These sessions serve as a living matrix of the shape of the profession and its interests. More sessions one year as opposed to previous years serves as evidence of growing interest in a topic; fewer sessions on a topic over the years attests to diminishing interest. And starting the program this year with a session on raising money says everything about the most urgent problem facing the profession: decreasing funding.

Over the years the convention and the organization have grown considerably in size and diversity. Back in 1889, when the seventh annual convention was held in Cambridge, Massachusetts, sixty-two people attended to hear nineteen presentations in five sessions along with a variety of reports. All of the members of the MLA at that time were men.

To highlight this fact, Charles W. Eliot, President of Harvard University, gave a welcome address to the association on Thursday night, and then invited "the members of the Association *and their wives"* to a reception at his home on 17 Quincy Street after the formal address to the organization by its president, the poet, James Russell Lowell. The 1889 program also explicitly notes "The attendance of Ladies at the Sessions of the Convention will be expected and welcomed." The twentieth-century though would bring major changes to the demographics of the MLA, not the least of which would be the steadily increasing role and status of women in the organization and the profession.

In 1989, one-hundred years later, the MLA Committee on the Status of Women in the Profession reported that about 48 percent of doctorates in English and 64 percent of doctorates in foreign languages that year were awarded to women. And of those doctorates in English, 656 were awarded to white women and 54 to women of color; of the doctorates in foreign languages, 180 were awarded to white women and 34 to women of color. Moreover, though the MLA president was male in 1989 (Victor Brombert), women held the position the year before (Barbara Herrnstein Smith, 1988) and the year after (Catherine R. Stimpson, 1990). In addition, since 1985, the three executive directors of the MLA have all been women (Phyllis Franklin, 1985-2002; Rosemary G. Feal, 2002-2017; and Paula M. Krebs, 2017-present).

Furthermore, a 1995 Survey of Humanities Doctorates conducted by the National Opinion Research Center reported that among Assistant Professors of English, approximately 16 percent were white men, 23 percent were white women, 22 percent were men of color, and 34 percent were women of color; among Assistant Professors of Foreign Languages, approximately 14 percent were white men, 26 percent were white women, 16 percent were men of color, and 31 percent were women of color. Nevertheless, at the highest rank, there were wide disparities based on gender and minority status. Full Professors of English were about 46 percent white men, 22 percent were white women, 27 percent were men of color, and 24 percent were women of color; among Full Professors of Foreign Languages, approximately 50 percent were white men, 19 percent were white women, 42 percent were men of color, and 13 percent were women of color.

The profession and the organization have come a long way in the past one hundred years in terms of diversity and conference programming—much more so than the profession of philosophy and its national organization, the American Philosophical Association (APA), which throughout the century until the present has been and continues to be predominantly white and male.

Until 2011, when the MLA Annual Convention meeting date was changed from three days after Christmas (December 27-30) to four days after the start of the New Year (January 6-9), it was always held on the same three days as the APA's Annual Eastern Division Convention. As a member of both organizations, through the winter of 2009, I would spend a day at the MLA and a day at the APA. The contrast between the two organization's annual meetings could not have been more drastic: from the differing demographics of the groups to the style, content, and tone of the sessions, one group appeared to be from Venus and the other from Mars.

However, if one thing definitively set the APA apart from the MLA it was the "smoker." This was the common space of the convention where philosophy department search committees would sit in the evening at tables in a large room while prospective job applicants and their advocates would move from table to table in an effort to secure the applicants a position. As the night wore on, the smoke from the philosopher's pipes, cigars, and cigarettes would engulf the room in a grey haze. Hence the term, "smoker."

But APA smokers are not for everyone. In an anonymous blog post a few years ago, "What It Is Like to Be a Woman in Philosophy," someone wrote "APA interviewing . . . means spending several nights up late, standing in uncomfortable shoes in a hotel ballroom, sipping cranberry juice while talking to tipsy prospective employers at that monstrosity we call the 'smoker.'" The anonymous poster also said that "the setting of the smoker is overwhelming proof of the maleness of the profession, and that one time she was at the smoker before, she was hit on." Though APA figures set the number of women in the profession at around twenty-five to twenty-eight percent, the continuation of annual hiring process rituals like the smoker makes it feel significantly less, especially for women in philosophy.

Given then the demographics of the MLA versus the APA membership, it is not much of a reach to say that the MLA is a much more diverse organization. It is also a much larger one too. In 2018, the MLA had 26,384 members, whereas in the same year, the APA had 8,266.

From its inception in 1883 until 1930, attendance at the MLA convention though was not exceedingly large. It would not be until 1930 that attendance would break one thousand for the first time (with 1,107 attending that year), and by its annual meeting in New York City on December 28-30, 1948, its attendance reached an all-time organization high with 3,049 participants. The next year, however, there were only 852 attendees for the 1949 meeting at Stanford University—the lowest attendance since the 1933 meeting in St. Louis where there were only 563 attendees.

Still between 1952 and 2019, attendance at the MLA would never be lower than 2,555 (1952). It went over 5,000 attendees for the first time in 1962 (5,550) and over 10,000 attendees for the first time in 1966 (10,600), and peaked attendance in 1968 with 11,750. From 1969 to 2019 attendance fluctuated between 4,500 (Houston, 1980) and 11,700 (New York, 1992). Attendance for the 2018 meeting in New York City was 6,040. By comparison, the 2018 APA Eastern Division meeting in Savannah, Georgia had just over one thousand participants listed in the program.

æ

Unlike 1889, where all of the participants had the opportunity to hear all of the MLA presentations, today this is no longer possible. Seven hundred and forty-seven sessions over four days mean there are many concurrent sessions. There are of course a few sessions such as the Presidential Address that do not conflict with other sessions, but none of the conference venues are prepared for the possibility of all of the attendees going to it. Even in New York City, where Radio City Music Hall seats 5,933 and the Hulu Theater at Madison Square Garden seats up to 5,600, there would not be a venue large enough for all conference participants to attend a presentation short of the Garden itself which seats 20,000 for concerts.

If the presentations including the Presidential and plenary are not the common space of the MLA conference, and as the MLA does not have anything like the APA's "smoker," then what is it? As anyone who has ever attended the MLA in the last half-century will tell you, it is the book exhibition. It is the place one goes to meet old acquaintances, to check out the latest books in the field, and to pitch book ideas with editors. Whether it is an old friend, a new book, or an editor, there is something there for everyone. It is our profession's annual carnival albeit one that has over the years featured fewer and fewer exhibitors.

Fifty years ago, there were 119 exhibitors at the 1969 meeting. In 1970, the following year, there were 114 exhibitors. Flash-forward to 1980, and the number of exhibitors drops even further to 101. But by 1990, the number rises to 136 exhibitors. By 2000, however, it goes down to 120 exhibitors—almost the exact number of exhibitors as thirty years earlier. Exhibitor attrition starts to become acute though in the years following the U.S. market collapse with only 84 exhibitors in 2009 and a mere 77 exhibitors in 2019. If the formative years of your MLA book exhibit experience were the 1990s like mine, then one saw a lot of tumbleweed where there were once booths at the January 2019 MLA book exhibit. But what was its source? What exhibitors were bailing? The answer here is a bit surprising.

Back in 1969 and 1970, of the many exhibitors, only 27 and 26 were respectively university presses. The rest of the exhibiting publishers were trade, independent, and small presses. By 1980, the number of university presses slipped to 23. However, in 1990, the number of university presses at the MLA Book Exhibition more than doubled, reaching 55. In 2000, though that number dipped to 44 but has plateaued since with 35 university presses at the 2009 MLA Book Exhibition and 37 in the past two years (2018 and 2019). This means that over the past fifty years, in spite of some fluctuations, the number of university presses exhibiting at the MLA *has risen by 37 percent* even though the number of overall exhibitors *has decreased by 35 percent.*

The picture then of our annual book exhibition looks different depending on what set of data one chooses to feature: on the one hand, the MLA Book Exhibition has decreased in size by 35 percent over the past half century; on the other hand, the number of university presses exhibiting at the annual conference has increased by 37 percent.

These numbers get even more interesting when one considers that the Association of University Presses currently has around 140 members world-wide, whereas the number of U.S. mass-market and trade publishers has been estimated to be 58,795. If this figure were not large enough, consider too that the Bowker database has about 85,000 publishers with active ISBNs. Of these 85,000 publishers

81

only twelve of them account for nearly two-thirds of all U.S. trade and mass-market book sales. And it is easy to find their booths at the MLA—just look for the double- and triple-wides.

But my point here is not to bash corporate publishers for exhibiting at the MLA. Rather, it is to point out that without the consistent and increasing support of university presses over the past fifty years, the MLA Book Exhibition would be all tumbleweed.

Or, perhaps, *all digital* like the "real" MLA Commons, a website built and maintained by the organization so that it is easier for scholars to work together and communicate about their research and teaching, to connect with their colleagues, to voice their opinions, to get MLA news updates, and to take part in group discussions. Among the many features that the MLA Commons encourages you to explore to "help with your particular goals, needs, and interests," is one that allows you to "Take control of your online presence and present your work [to] the world at large with a networked WordPress Web site hosted by the *Commons*."

Scary as it may sound, isn't the next logical step for the MLA to develop a digital book exhibition for its annual conference? For one thing, it would arguably serve a larger proportion of its membership as decreasing numbers of members are attending the annual conference. For another, it would allow more publishers to be included in the book exhibition as presumably the cost of exhibiting in this digital MLA book exhibition would be less prohibitive. If our "real" MLA Commons is a digital one, then it might make sense as well to turn our annual conference commons—the book exhibition— into a purely digital affair.

Aside from the incredibly shrinking MLA Book Exhibition, there were also noticeably fewer people at the conference this year.[3] One of the reasons is that many universities and colleges are doing their job interviews through Zoom, Skype, or some other digital platform to save the expense and time of convening a committee and candidates at the MLA. Fewer job interviews led to fewer participants at the conference. In turn, this meant fewer folks taking part in the organization's annual book carnival.

Those university presses that remain committed to the Annual MLA Convention should be cherished by those who enjoy running into old acquaintances, leafing through the latest books in the field, and pitching book ideas with university press editors. For without the steadfast and increasing support of these presses over the past fifty years, our annual convention might have lost its commons by now.

Think about this the next time you go to the MLA book exhibition. Or get angry because one of your favorite university presses is running into financial trouble and on the verge of closure. And as we have seen of late, it is not just the smaller university presses that are under threat of closure or reduction of financial support, but the larger ones as well. University of Missouri, Northwestern University Press, University of California Press, and now Stanford University Press have all been recently financially challenged by their respective universities. And Eastern Washington University, Southern Methodist University, and the University of Scranton Presses were closed. However, *all* of the university presses who exhibited at the 1969 and 1970 MLA Conventions are still publishing scholarly books fifty years later. Maybe it is because participating in the MLA Book Exhibition is the secret to university press longevity—in addition to being the organization's *real* commons.

10 | WAX POWER

The advent of vinyl records was paved by a fifty-year journey that began with a stylus reading a groove on a wax cylinder.

Thomas Edison's phonograph, which converts the wax cylinder's grooves into sound via a diaphragm, was developed in 1877. The first sound recording played back on the phonograph was Edison mouthing the words, "Mary had a little lamb."

The first commercially available vinyl long-playing records were produced by RCA in 1931. But prior to 1958, there were no commercially available sound recordings in stereo. That would all change though when the record company, Audio Fidelity, previewed a "stereo" long-playing recording at the Times Auditorium in New York City on December 13, 1957.

On one side of the LP was a stereo recording of the Dukes of Dixieland jazz band, and on the other, were railroad sound effects from steam and diesel locomotives. The initial print run was 500 records, and Audio Fidelity offered free copies through an advertisement in *Billboard* magazine to anyone in the music industry that asked for one. Then, on December 13, 1957, they introduced the first-ever commercial recordings in stereophonic two-channel sound—and by the end of 1958, stereo LPs would be commercially available by every major record label.

In one sense, the story of sound recording begins with Edison's words, and moves through nearly one-hundred and fifty years of sound recording development from wax cylinders and vinyl records to compact discs and MP3s. The standard tale here is one of increasing levels of sound fidelity with events like the staging of stereophonic sound with railroad sound effects marking significant progress in sound fidelity. It is the story of a journey from the low fidelity of the gramophone to the high fidelity of the compact disc.

However, in another, more philosophical sense, the invention and development of the phonograph marks a very late stage in the development of sound recording—a journey that dates back to a power first attributed only to the gods.

What brings together both the story of the early stages of sound recording and the story of its later stages is the general idea that *power comes through the ability to control sound in society*. My term for this form of power is "wax power."

ॐ

The ancient gods were said to have three essential powers: making war, causing famine, and recording sound. This might seem like an odd triumvirate of powers, particularly the latter power, but imagine a world where there is no means to store information other than memory. The sounds that we make to each other in discourse, and those that we hear in the world around us, can only be repeated and passed along to others through acts of memory.

It is somewhat fitting then that when the ancient Greek philosopher, Plato, discussed memory in his philosophical dialogue *Theaetetus*, he asked us to imagine it in one sense as a "block of wax, which in this or that individual may be larger or smaller, and composed of wax that is comparatively pure or muddy, and harder in some, softer in others, and sometimes just the right consistency."

"Let us call it," says Plato,

> the gift of the Muses' mother, Memory, and say that whenever we wish to remember something we see or hear or conceive in our own minds, we hold this wax under the perceptions or ideas and imprint on it as we might stamp the impression of a seal ring. Whatever is so imprinted we remember and know so long as the image remains; whatever is rubbed out or has not succeeded in leaving an impression we have forgotten and do not know.

Though the imprinting of perceptions or ideas on wax here has more in common with block printing than a stylus making sound impressions on soft wax, the notion that this act might be regarded as "the gift" of a god to humankind assumes that the actual power of total memory is one held by the gods—and not humankind.

Plato also says that Homer too struggles to explain human memory, and "hints at the mind's likeness to wax." He attributes to Homer the view that "When a man has in his mind a good thick slab of wax, smooth and kneaded to the right consistency . . . the impressions that come through the senses are stamped on [the] tables of the 'heart.'"

Wax then for thinkers following the leads of Homer and Plato embodies the potential of sound recording—a potential that is ironically or perhaps even fittingly—first fulfilled in the late nineteenth century by Edison by means of the self-same medium: wax. The implication then that the Muses' mother, Memory, has a mind of perfectly constituted wax that preserves all recorded sound offers us one way to understand how recorded sound as memory might be regarded as a godly power in ancient civilizations.

ॐ

But still, set next to the power to create war and cause famine, that is, to take away life, doesn't the biopower of recorded sound pale in comparison? Wars and famines are the instruments of death and destruction where the fate of life is always precarious. The gods have the abilities to both give life and take it away, and these powers in the form of inflicting war and famine upon humankind are their most awesome and fear inducing. Given the biopower of war and famine, might we expect outcomes of a similar order to also be attributed to those with the ability to record sound?

First of all, without the ability to record sound it would be very difficult to have any reliable information—that is, "knowledge"—of the past including knowledge of past wars and famines. Indeed, the context of Plato's comments on the waxen nature of memory were part of a more general effort to define knowledge. Recorded sound gives us the ability to know, for example, that the first war in recorded history took place in Mesopotamia in 2700 BCE between Sumer and Elam, and that one of the first famines on record occurred from 2770-2730 BCE during the reign of the Egyptian pharaoh Djeser. We also know through recorded sound that this ancient famine was caused by the failure of the Nile to break its banks seven years in a row. Knowledge of these events and others from history are only possible because they have been passed down to us through early sound recording.

However, it is also certain that there were wars caused by humankind before the one that took place in Mesopotamia in 2700 BCE, but because there is no record of them, we have no knowledge of them.

87

Same too with famines, both those caused by natural circumstances such as drought and those deliberately engineered to kill. In fact, we know through recorded sound that in the ancient Greco-Roman world, siege-induced famines were not unusual, and that military manuals explained how to poison water reservoirs and destroy food supplies. These records show, for example, that Julius Caesar, used a siege-induced famine to conquer Vercingetorix's Gauls at Alesia in 52 BCE. It is important to remember in this context that Caesar made a habit of recording his military conquests from the field and sending these reports back to Rome as a way of building his power in the Republic.

Moreover, the line between knowledge of the past and its absence is in large measure marked by the ability to record sound. Therefore, our knowledge of the time before the invention of the cuneiform script, the first writing, in Mesopotamia (which is now called Iraq) in 3200 BCE is very limited. The pre-historic era is thus generally set as ending around the time of the invention of writing, or for our purposes, around the time of the invention of sound recording. And while the oldest known cave paintings are said to be 40,000 years old, and predate by far the invention of sound recording, their power is of a different order than that of early sound recordings. While these pre-historic cave paintings are amazingly beautiful art, they do not provide much more knowledge of the past than fossils and bones excavated from the ground.

≥▲

The ability then of the gods to record sound is the ability to know the history of the world in its totality back to its beginnings—and with this knowledge comes great power. By comparison, the scattered fragments recorded in history books or recounted from generation to generation pale. Recording though is important not just because it provides us with a more extensive knowledge of the past, but also because these records can be used as a means of social and political *control*. In fact, the French theorist Jacques Attali goes so far as to propose "Recording has *always been* a means of social control, a stake in politics, regardless of the available technologies."

"Always," of course, does not mean "forever," but rather refers to the five-thousand-year history of recording. It is a period that extends backwards from the digital recording of the present through Edison's invention of sound recording and the recorded histories of ancient Greece and Rome back to the cuneiform script of Mesopotamia. During this period, the period of "recording," writes Attali,

> Power is no longer content to enact its legitimacy; it records and reproduces the societies it rules. Stockpiling memory, retaining history or time, distributing speech, and manipulating information has always been an attribute of civil and priestly power, beginning with the Tables of the Law.

Ancient lore has it too that the necessity and power of recording sound increased as the bond of the verbal contract began to weaken and break down. Recording provided more assurance that contracts and agreements between parties would be honored, and thus increased the level of control in society.

ह

Still, the amount of social and political control available through recording was relatively limited compared to what occurred *after* Edison's invention. Attali comments that "before the industrial age," recording

> did not occupy center stage: Moses stuttered and it was Aaron who spoke. But there was already no mistaking: the reality of power belonged to he who was able to reproduce the divine word, not to he who gave it voice on a daily basis.

But with Edison's invention and the advances in sound recording that followed, *power came through the ability to control sound in society.* "Possessing the means of recording allows one to monitor noises, to maintain them, and to control their repetition within a determined code," writes Attali. "In the final analysis, it allows one to impose one's own noise and to silence others," he continues. Attali then directly follows this comment with a chilling quote from Adolf Hitler from the *Manual of German Radio* published in 1938: "Without the loudspeaker, we would never have conquered Germany."

Radio though is not a means of sound recording. Still, it is a primary means of sound control and, used appropriately, a vehicle of power, especially in the first half of the twentieth century. Fittingly, the same year as Hitler's remark about the controlling power of radio, Adorno would move from England, where he had been living since fleeing National Socialism in Germany in 1934, to New York City for the purpose of working at the Princeton Radio Research Project.

Though it was not Adorno's aim at the time to either leave Europe or to write extensively on radio, the Princeton Radio Research Project, which provided Adorno with a funded position, gave Max Horkheimer, who set up the opportunity, a way to bring Adorno to New York City. From his arrival in New York City in February of 1938 through November of 1941, when funding for his position was not renewed, Adorno wrote extensively on radio. His major work from this period, *Current of Music: Elements of a Radio Theory*, was left unfinished at his death though has recently been reconstructed and published.

I mention Adorno's work here because in *Current of Music* and elsewhere he comments on the ways in which sound recording affects music. In *Current of Music*, his express topic is how radio transmission transforms our perception of music. His critical physiognomy of live radio music, while less savage than his critique of phonographic music, is still highly negative of the emancipatory potential for music transmitted by radio. He sees both as "steps in the mechanization of musical production," which he views as destroying "authenticity" in music:

> Now, we believe that *this* authenticity, or aura, is vanishing in music because of mechanical reproduction. The phonograph record destroys the "now" of the live performance and, in a way, its "here" as well. Although the ubiquity of radio observes the "now," it certainly is more hostile to the "here."

For Adorno, music and our perception of it changed in the age of mechanical reproduction, albeit not for the better. Music became both a commodity and an industry through its mechanical reproduction. Nevertheless, Adorno does not take the social, political, and economic implications of recording sound as far as Attali, who argues that the phonographic record brought about a "new" economy. It is an economic order that we have come to term "late capitalism" or "neoliberalism." According to Attali, this new economy grew in strength as the record industry expanded and developed over the course of the twentieth century. Vinyl records came to be the harbingers of the neoliberal political economy.

In short, the prospects of wax power from the perspective of theorists like Adorno and Attali attribute to vinyl unexpected and unforeseen economic and political powers.

Wax power allows us to consider the stylus as both a central tool of neoliberalism and the contemporary hammer of the gods.

11 | A FIG LEAF FOR LITERATURE

Many are worried about the future of literature. It is a nagging worry that only seems to worsen over time. This worry comes not from those who can't tell the difference between Dante and Dostoevsky. For them, literature is neither an object of affection nor a window to the world. It is a door within the house of knowledge that they cannot bring themselves to open. Rather, the worry mainly comes from those most familiar with literature. For scholars and admirers of literature who have explored its long history dating back thirty-three centuries to the Gilgamesh epic. For them, a most fatal concern has arisen of late: the real possibility of the emergence of a post-literature era.

The worry is not that there will be some massive fire like the one in Alexandria where vast amounts of literature are lost forever. Future generations will have even greater access to the literature of the world that has been passed down through the millennia. Nor is the worry that there will not be a coterie of scholars who will continue to study it for many years to come. Even the most ardent proponents of a decreased role for literature in the university do not believe that its study will or should disappear entirely. Rather, the worry is that what will happen to the study of literature is what happened to the study of Greek and Latin in the academy. Whereas a century ago, the study of classical languages was the mark of an educated person and a sign of a complete university education, today it is regarded as a non-essential, educational "luxury" item.

Just as the study of Greek and Latin in the twentieth century was an expiring holdover from the nineteenth century, the study of literature might be viewed in the twenty-first century as an expiring holdover from the twentieth century. Whether it is because literature is linked to an outmoded technology or because there is less sustained reading attention or whatever, there is a strong feeling that literature is being traded out today for something different. We might disagree about the specifics of these trades, but the fact that they are being made with increasing frequency seems obvious to most scholars and admirers of literature.

While some contend that declining interest in the book compared to other technologies of communication such as television, film, and the Internet is linked to the declining future of literature, there are others who lay the blame entirely within the academy. These folks believe that fifty or so years ago the academy began the process of trading literature for theory. Supposedly, there was a time before the linguistic turn when professors and students studied literature, not the structure of language. The legacies of structuralism and poststructuralism brought about a turning away from literature, and replaced it with literary and cultural theory.

Last gasp efforts to purge theory from the university and recuperate literature in its wake such as postcritique and surface reading only serve to exacerbate our worries about literature lost rather than quell them. Moreover, finding a new theory to recuperate literature in the academy after it has been effectively marginalized leads some to wrongly assume that *theory* was the principle cause of the declining value of literature in the academy—and not something else.

It is highly unlikely that "the hermeneutics of suspicion" led students to not want to study literature for nine out ten don't even know what it is. Students learn about theory through the study of literature, and learn about literature through the study of theory. If anything, theory kept literature in the university on life-support for longer than it would have been without it. Rather, academics began the process of trading literature when the university aimed to become a vocational training center. What we traded literature for were all of those other areas of study that allegedly make students better prepared for their vocation and the workforce. Business majors had no business studying Beckett, and Montaigne and Marlowe were traded for management and marketing courses. In short, the study of world literature was traded for workforce learning.

Thus, for today's average student, studying comparative literature is comparable only to seeking the most efficient means of underemployment. And in spite of the impassioned manifestos by earnest and learned literature professors that the study of literature will get you a better job upon graduation than those who don't study literature, this is a type of argument that is always born to lose in the neoliberal academy. The rising cost of education is indeed both monetary and intellectual. Students have traded the study of literature for the pursuit of a better future through vocational training.

The balance of trade regarding literature has resulted in a vicious circle where literature is increasingly diminished with each trade-off. Students don't want to study literature because they believe it is not going to provide them with a secure financial future, and professors don't want to teach literature because their students don't want to study it. Few things are more painful for faculty than trying to convince students that their time and money is not being wasted through the study of topics they regard as superfluous.

The rise of the neoliberal vision of the university has decimated its academic ideals and replaced them with the protocols of debt culture and market economics. While it was possible once to make the utilitarian case that studying literature provides the skills needed to be successful in your life and career, this can no longer be achieved. The professional training model of higher education which places a high value on curricular efficiency and educational instrumentality now runs deep in the veins of the public imagination.

To be sure, a trade imbalance regarding literature exists in the university today. It has come about because far too many students, faculty, and administrators have chosen to trade literature and the higher aims of education away. Similar shameful trade-offs too have been made in other areas such as philosophy and rhetoric. To trade away work that has been a central part of the academy since its origins in ancient Greece, and literature that dates back even earlier, is ultimately to trade away higher education for a much lower and inferior version.

Perhaps the only way to hide our shame in trading literature for vocational training is to cover it with the fig leaf of post-literature. But what does this mean? Doing so allows us to lay the blame for trading literature in the academy not on neoliberal academe, but rather on the advancements in technology that have resulted in a decrease in the sustained readerly-attention that literature has traditionally demanded. The post-literature world is one where reading attention is not required for the new forms of writing that are emerging in the wake of traditional forms of literature.

95

The novelist, Robert Coover, describes this post-literature world as one where we "will continue, in whatever medium and with whatever tools, to tell stories, explore paradox, strive for meaning and beauty (those sweet old illusions), pursue self-understanding, seek out the hidden content of the tribal life, and so on—in short, all the grand endeavors we associate with literature, even if what they make may not be literature, any more than film is literature or nature a poem." This post-literature world is the mirror image of the post-university world, or what we now commonly refer to as *the neoliberal academy*.

If the post-literature world is one where we traded literature for something else that nonetheless allows us to continue "all the grand endeavors we associate with literature," then the neoliberal academy is one where we traded education for something else that nonetheless allows us to continue "all the grand endeavors we associate with *education*." Though this is a dark mirror image, it is a fitting one for dark times. More importantly, though it leaves our worries about the future of literature intact, it is a dark mirror image that mitigates at least some of our responsibility as literature professors for the trading away of our livelihood.

෴

But there is still another meaning to covering our shame in trading literature for vocational training by covering it with the *fig leaf* of post-literature. It is a meaning that does not mitigate our responsibility. Instead, it places it squarely upon our shoulders as willing participants in the curricular trade economy of higher education. This meaning can be traced back to David Hume's essay "Of the Balance of Trade," which was first published in 1752. In it, he writes in support of free trade among nations and warns against prohibitions to exporting certain commodities. "In it very usual, in nations ignorant of the nature of commerce," writes Hume, "to prohibit the exportation of commodities, and to preserve among themselves whatever they think valuable and useful." "They do not consider, that, in the prohibition, they act directly contrary to their intention; and that the more is exported of any commodity, the more will be raised at home, of which they themselves will always have the first offer."

To illustrate the dangers of prohibiting trade, Hume uses the example of ancient Greek law that prohibited the exportation of figs:

It is well known to the learned, that the ancient laws of Athens rendered the exportation of figs criminal; that being supposed a species of fruit so excellent in Attica, that the Athenians deemed it too delicious for the palate of any foreigner.

But the prohibition on fig exportation is only half of the story. The other half concerns the economy and politics of informing on those who exported figs. The Greeks had a specific term for such informers, "sycophant." Again, Hume:

> And in this ridiculous prohibition they were so much in earnest that informers were thence called *sycophants* among them, from two Greek words, which signify *figs* and *discoverer.*

Whereas now the term "sycophant" generally refers to a servile self-seeking flatterer, in ancient Greece, the term generally refers to a "public informer"—the Greek counterpart of the Roman "delator."

While it is a combination of the Greek words for "fig" and "to show," there is much debate as to the meaning of "sycophant." For some, the word simply refers to those who inform against others for stealing the fruit of the "sacred" fig tree or exporting it. But for others, because taxes and fines were at one time in ancient Greece paid in wine, oil, and figs, the word "sycophant" refers to those who handed over fines and taxes to the state. Another meaning attributed to the term is as an "obscene gesture of phallic significance" called "showing the fig" directed toward another for some frivolous or trivial reason. On this meaning, the sycophant is the person who initiates the insult. There is also a meaning of the term that connects it to the ancient Greek cult of the Phytalidae, wherein a "sycophant" was an official connected with the cult. Phytalus, the namesake of the cult, was rewarded a fig tree by Demeter in return for the hospitality he provided to the wanderer.

The darkest meaning though from antiquity links the term to those who blackmail others over their "figs" (or money). In this sense, a sycophant is someone who threatens to bring criminal charges against a rich person, that is, someone with a wealth of figs, unless they pay off the sycophant not to press the criminal charges. In Athens, any citizen could at any time accuse another of a public offense. As those

97

in positions of power and wealth were looked upon with suspicion by the Athenian citizens, many were willing to believe most any charge brought against the rich and powerful. This made wealthy individuals vulnerable to blackmail by sycophants.

What is interesting is that despite the potential for sycophants to blackmail the rich and the powerful or even to bring false charges against them, they were nonetheless regarded as an essential part of Athenian democracy. Moreover, the profession of sycophant was not regarded as a dishonorable one. The practice of encouraging citizens to help in the detection of crimes against the state was important even if some abused the opportunity for personal gain.

Hume does us a service by reminding us of the historical connection between prohibitions to free trade and sycophants—even if he is critical of such prohibitions, calling them "ridiculous" and "errors, one may say, [that are] gross and palpable." The *fig-leaf* of post-literature that we took early as one of "shame" for trading literature for vocational training comes to mean through the perspective of Hume on free trade and the Greeks on sycophancy something quite different. It is a meaning that is much darker than "shame" and may be directly linked to the political economy of neoliberalism.

As participants in the neoliberal university who are concerned about the future of literature, we are encouraged to be sycophants in the classical sense. When the university veers from its vocational telos, we are encouraged to report though curricular assessment the deviation. For those who are passionate advocates of literature but cannot link the teaching of literature to the vocational ends of the university, it can be difficult to become a "literature informer" for the neoliberal university. But what else can we do?

Our prohibited goods are not figs but literature. The humanities would like to keep them all for themselves, and resist exporting them to the professional sides and ends of the academic house. As I've argued before, this is not a healthy practice for the economy of the humanities in the age of neoliberal academe. Students with vocational aspirations who are careerists are radically altering humanities education in America—and the humanities curriculum is slowly giving way to their vocational and corporate interests. How then do we meet the demands of these vocationally-motivated students while at the same time resist trading away literature instruction in our curriculum? This of course is one the central challenges facing the future of literature in the neoliberal university.

To be sure, we cannot and should not ignore or denigrate the desires of our vocationally-directed students. Rather, we need to engage them in a progressive form of dialogue with and through the literature courses that we do offer. "Vocationalizing" or "corporatizing" literature courses however does not mean that we ignore the historical and political dimensions of the works that we are teaching, rather it means that we need to be careful not to assume that our students *prima facia* care about the critical foundations of texts or even literature itself. Teaching literature courses in this context requires a more complex dialogue between teacher and students in order to respect mutual desires. In the end, however, this respect of different desires may be one of the only ways to prevent the eventual extinction of large swaths of the liberal arts curriculum—especially if our corporate liberal arts courses bring about a greater knowledge of and appreciation for the liberal arts.

The curriculum of the university is a political economy. Prohibiting the free exchange of ideas within the university by prohibiting—or at least discouraging—instruction in key areas human knowledge such as literature, philosophy, and rhetoric will result in negative consequences for the university and the society to which it aims to benefit. Hume's warning about the Greeks and their figs is analogous to the situation today of the university and literature. Shame turns to fear when the fig leaf is now hiding the decimation of not just literature but also the destruction of the university too. On this bleaker reading of the post-literature world, when we traded literature for vocational training, we did far more than hide our shame with the fig leaf of post-literature. We also became sycophants in the classical sense: namely, literature "informers" in the darkest senses of the classical term.

99

12 | FASHIONABLE PHILOSOPHY

Theory entered the academy in the late 1960s—and philosophy has been at odds with it ever since.

From the perspective of philosophy, theory is *their* thing. The term itself can be traced back to ancient Greek philosophy where thinkers like Xenophanes and Aristotle coined its historical role in Western thought.

William James, a professor of philosophy at Harvard University from 1880 to 1889 and 1897 to 1907 (he was on the psychology faculty during the middle period), wrote in his final book, *Some Problems of Philosophy* (1911), "every generation of men produces some individuals exceptionally preoccupied with theory." "Such men," he continues,

> find matter for puzzle and astonishment where no one else does. Their imagination invents explanations and combines them. They store up the learning of their time, utter prophecies and warnings, and are regarded as sages.

For James, this theoretical work is the work of philosophy, something he regards as an essential part of a liberal education. "Philosophy," wrote James, "indeed, in one sense of the term is only a compendious name for the spirit in education which the word 'college' stands for in America."

The story of how theory came to be at odds with philosophy in the late twentieth-century is a sad one. James had a pluralistic view of philosophy, one where many different theoretical approaches to the problems that interest us are a key part of the academy. "To know the chief rival attitudes towards life, as the history of human thinking has developed them, and to have heard some of the reasons they can give for themselves," said James, "ought to be considered an essential part of liberal education." One hundred years later though this vision of a liberal education has been lost. Part of the reason is that philosophy in the academy lost its pluralistic spirit.

❧

Late twentieth-century theory was not the *theoria* of antiquity.

Though there are a number of senses of theory, such as the idea that theory is the "methods" of literary studies; that theory is a collection of schools or movements; that theory is a flexible toolbox of concepts; and that theory is just what every specialist knows, one particular idea of theory stood above them all and came to be theory's central signifier: the somewhat narrow structuralist and poststructuralist high-theory notion.

In the late '60s and early '70s, structuralist and poststructuralist thought came to be regarded as the "linguistic turn." It would have a profound and revolutionary impact on the human sciences including literary studies and philosophy. Not only did theory challenge the critical model of the New Criticism then fashionable in English departments, it also had a ripple effect in philosophy departments, which were then largely divided along analytic and continental lines.

Whereas English departments were relatively quick to absorb the fruits of the linguistic turns of structuralism and poststructuralism into their curriculums and scholarship, philosophy departments had the opposite reaction. Instead of widely embracing the linguistic turn, the roots of which lay deep in the philosophical tradition, they used it as an opportunity to further widen the analytic and continental divide in philosophy.

Whereas prior to the linguistic turn, continental philosophy from the perspective of the American philosophy department largely involved phenomenology, existentialism, and the Frankfurt school, after the linguistic turn it expanded to include structuralism and poststructuralism. By the close of the twentieth-century, though the continental philosophies of Jacques Lacan, Julia Kristeva, Hélène Cixous, Jean-François Lyotard, Gilles Deleuze, Michel Foucault, and Jacques Derrida, and others, were an important part of the American higher educational curriculum with many professors producing scholarship in this area, it was largely not due to the efforts of its philosophy departments, which widely refused to teach the work in this area or even to recognize it as "good" philosophy. Instead, the rise of theory in the academy was largely due to its adoption by English, comparative literature, and foreign language departments.

The reason for this is that philosophy in America in the late-twentieth century was still on a course laid out a century earlier when it came to be bitten by the scientific progress bug. The irony here is that this "bug" came to American philosophy in the late nineteenth century via developments on earlier work from the continent by English philosophers such as Francis Bacon, William Whewell, and J. S. Mill by American philosophers such as Charles S. Peirce and William James for whom the scientific method came to mean experimental empiricism.

This change was occurring while other important American philosophers, such as Henry David Thoreau and Ralph Waldo Emerson, the latter of whom famously called for a break from the continental traditions as early as 1837 in his justly celebrated divinity school address, "The American Scholar," were starting to be ignored by mainstream philosophers and philosophy departments—a course that would intensify such that by the close of the twentieth century their work was primarily relegated for study only in English departments, which were also home to much of the work of theory.

Moreover, if not for the influential contributions of the late twentieth-century Harvard philosopher, Stanley Cavell, whose work brought Emerson and Thoreau into conversation with Ludwig Wittgenstein, J. L. Austin, and others, these philosophers would probably have an ever smaller role in United States philosophy departments today, who, for the most part, relegate their work merely to historical surveys of American philosophy. That is to say, to the curricular dustbin of philosophical ideas.

≈

Twentieth-century analytic philosophy found in the conceptual analysis of G. E. Moore and logical atomism (and logical-analytic pluralism) of Bertrand Russell a methodology that could mirror the exactitude and certainty of the sciences. Logical empiricism rejected metaphysics as unverifiable, and focused instead on perfecting conceptual analysis.

In addition, analytic philosophers had their own "linguistic turn." It was not one that revolved around the work of structuralism and poststructuralism, but rather one that involved the aforementioned logical empiricism in addition to American pragmatism and ordinary language philosophy.

103

If Ferdinand de Saussure's *Cours de Linguistique Générale* (1916) is considered the foundational text of theory's linguistic turn, then Ludwig Wittgenstein's *Tractatus Logico-Philosophicus* (1921) is the foundational text of philosophy's linguistic turn.

The expression "the linguistic turn" was first introduced in analytic philosophy in a review of Peter Strawson's book *Individuals* in 1960 by Gustav Bergmann. The neopragmatist Richard Rorty popularized the name among philosophers when he edited the book *The Linguistic Turn* in 1967.

The first part of Rorty's book contains classic statements on the thesis that philosophical questions are questions of language with contributions by Bergmann, Moritz Schlick, Rudolph Carnap, Gilbert Ryle, John Wisdom, and Norman Malcolm. The book also has major sections on the problem of ideal language philosophy including essays by Irving Copi and W. V. O. Quine, and ordinary language philosophy including essays by Roderick Chisholm and Stanley Cavell. In short, this group of philosophers and approach came through Bergmann and Rorty to be analytic philosophy's "linguistic turn," one very different than the project of structuralism and poststructuralism.

In the twentieth century, analytic philosophy and its linguistic turn dominated the institution of philosophy in America. Its stranglehold over professional philosophy in the United States was so strong that it led to one of the most significant rebellions in the history of the American Philosophical Association (APA). Led by Bruce W. Wilshire, a group of metaphysicians, continental, and pragmatic philosophers in the early 1970s demanded that the APA not treat their work as second-rate to the dominant analytic philosophy and include more of it in their conference programs. The work of this so-called "pluralist movement" eventually changed the APA to be more inclusive of "non-analytic" philosophy in their conference program and laid the course for its inclusion as well as the work of women and racial and ethnic minorities in APA conference programming.

In 2002, Wilshire published *Fashionable Nihilism: A Critique of Analytic Philosophy*, where he openly challenged analytic philosophy's detachment from everyday life. Wilshire called for professional philosophy to be more meaningful in our lives and to pursue the perennial questions that we face as human beings in our everyday existence. He did so not at the exclusion of the project of analytic philosophy, but rather as a complement to its "fashionable nihilism."

હ

But the problems regarding philosophical fashion pointed out by Wilshire were not new ones to philosophy in America. In fact, they can be traced back in the American philosophical tradition to the work of Emerson and Thoreau who fought hard against professional philosophy that excluded a role for philosophy in our lives.

Thoreau sums up well the problems facing philosophy in America in *Walden* (1854):

> There are nowadays professors of philosophy, but not philosophers. Yet it is admirable to profess because it was once admirable to live. To be a philosopher is not merely to have subtle thoughts, nor even to found a school, but so to love wisdom as to live according to its dictates, a life of simplicity, independence, magnanimity, and trust. It is to solve some of the problems of life, not only theoretically, but practically. The success of great scholars and thinkers is commonly a courtier-like success, not kingly, not manly.

Thoreau's distinction between a "professor of philosophy" and a "philosopher" is an important one because it suggests that we might make a distinction between academic philosophy, that is, what professors of philosophy pursue, and real philosophy, that is, what philosophers pursue. For Thoreau, the latter always involves an effort to solve some of the problems of everyday life, whereas the former is continuously beholden to the projects of professional philosophy as determined by their current fashion.

While there is no reason that professors of philosophy cannot pursue the problems of life, there is a lot of institutional history in the twentieth century that indicates that their major interests are found elsewhere. The roads determined by logical empiricism and analytic philosophy seldom led professional philosophers in America to the problems of life. Philosophical fashion in twentieth-century American philosophy was theoretically, not practically

105

oriented. This is contra, of course, to Thoreau's approach, where the theoretical and the practical work in combination toward solving the problems of life.

૨⁂

Just as the linguistic turn of analytic philosophy led to a late-twentieth century pluralist rebellion, so too did the linguistic turn of structuralism and poststructuralism albeit in a different way. Whereas academic philosophy opened its doors after their rebellion to a more diverse range of philosophical positions and issues, theory in the academy branched out to produce many new schools and movements in the wake of its "anti-theory rebellion" including feminism, race and gender studies, cultural studies, globalization studies, queer theory, postcolonialism, Marxism, and new historicism.

Today theory is a multi- and interdisciplinary endeavor that operates not just in the humanities, but also the sciences and the professions. A list of the various areas where it has branched out into "studies" includes everything from media and military science to education and environmental studies. In short, there are many more branches on the tree of theory than just structuralism and poststructuralism, and many work in their own way to identify and solve some of the problems of life.

For some, like me, this theoretical pluralism is one of the strengths of theory today. Like James, I think that learning the "chief rival attitudes towards life" brought to us by theory is an essential part of a liberal education. In fact, I would argue that the degree to which academe does not tolerate or encourage theoretical pluralism is the degree to which it fails with regard to a liberal education.

A liberal education provides students with both an introduction to a variety of theories or philosophies—as well as the tools to think and write critically about them. In a democratic and open society it is important that we learn how to think critically and deeply about our life as well as the lives of others. Theory provides us with the essential materials to carry this out in the university setting.

Philosophical fashion is nothing more or less than a name for the dominant philosophy of the day. For professional philosophers in America in the late twentieth century and early twenty-first century, it is analytic philosophy and its branches. Its problem with theory as pursued by structuralism and poststructuralism is that its theoretical genealogy comes from the wrong "linguistic turn."

The analytic "fashion" in professional philosophy has frequently led its non-pluralistic followers to disparage "theory" as "fashionable nonsense." Ammunition for their case has come from "hoaxes" like the one physics professor Alan Sokal did in 1996 when he published "Transgressing the Boundaries: Towards a Transformative Hermeneutics of Quantum Gravity" in the cultural studies journal *Social Text*. The fact that the journal published the hoax article and that its editorial collective included leading theorists such as Fredric Jameson and Andrew Ross allegedly "proved" to some that theory is merely fashionable nonsense.

Recently, another version of this type of hoax was planned and carried out by three authors—one of whom was a philosophy professor—who spent 10 months writing 20 hoax papers aimed at journals that publish work in the fields of gender, race, sexuality, and related fields. This so-called "Sokal Squared" hoax resulted in seven of the papers being accepted for publication with four published online and the other three set to be published before a *Wall Street Journal* editorial writer forced them to halt their project.

The aim of Sokal Squared was to question the work of scholars in the fields of gender, race, sexuality, and related areas, which they saw as "corrupting academic research." One of their "successes" was that not only was one of their papers published by the journal *Gender, Place & Culture*, it was also recognized for excellence by the journal. Though the article, "Expression of Concern: Human Reactions to Rape Culture and Queer Performativity at Urban Dog Parks in Portland, Oregon" was later retracted by the journal because the identity of its authors could not be verified, the hoaxers believed that its publication along with the others served to "expose the reality of grievance studies."

But while some find in the Sokal Affair and Sokal Squared a just desert for "fashionable nonsense," others see such efforts to "humiliate" entire fields of study including all of the students and faculty who participate in them as well as the universities with which they are affiliated as a reprehensible and flawed way to "improve" academic research.

It is reassuring though that this type of academic prank, that is, hoax articles aimed at humiliating fellow scholars and their areas of inquiry is not done more often. I think the fact that hoax articles aimed at humiliating people and their ideas are not commonplace in academe speaks to the pluralism and respect for others at the heart of scholarly inquiry today. Satire and hoaxes work well on late night television as a source of humor and a means of increasing viewership. But academe is not a late night television show. We have the more difficult task of learning how to disagree with each other without humiliating our peers.

Bruce Wilshire's name and university affiliation was on the cover of *Fashionable Nihilism*. The many analytic philosophers who hated his argument knew where to find him and they did, especially at APA meetings. To hide behind pseudonyms while attacking the efforts of scholars trying to make sense of gender, race, and sexuality in everyday life is not how members of the academy should engage in intellectual disagreement.

As the American Philosophical Association, the Modern Language Association, and related organizations are home to disagreements over the value of theory and the merits of analytic philosophy, they should discourage acts of public humiliation toward their members and journals. So too should those who believe in the value of intellectual pluralism and a liberal education. Fashionable philosophy will always draw the ire of rival positions, but there is always world enough for theoretical and practical debate regarding its merits without resorting to mean-spirited and deceitful behavior.

13 | DEAD CRITICISM

WITH A REPLY FROM HAROLD BLOOM

Harold Bloom is one of the most influential and prolific literary critics of his generation. A member of the Yale University English department since 1955, Bloom has taught legions of undergraduate and graduate students to appreciate literary greatness. In the process, he has published more than fifty books of literary criticism and appreciation since his first book, *Shelly's Mythmaking*, came out in 1959, and has edited hundreds of anthologies for Chelsea House publishing relating to literary and philosophical works and figures. He is a teacher, critic, and industry.

His latest book, *Possessed by Memory: The Inward Light of Criticism*, which it took him six years to write and was published a few months before he turns eighty-nine, is at once a condensation of many of his positions on literary greatness and influence, and a memorial to the many poets and critics that he considers his friends.[4] His declining health in recent years is well-chronicled in the volume as are the challenges it has presented to his teaching and writing. It is not uncommon in the volume to find lines from Bloom like "I dread falling every time I get up to walk" set next to long passages from Shakespeare or in this case, Proust.

It also not uncommon in the volume to find chapters that begin with a highly personal statement of where or when Bloom met a writer, and close with the personal impact of their death on Bloom. "I began to read John Ashbery's poetry in 1956, when I purchased *Some Trees* in a New Haven bookstore" opens a chapter that closes with

I loved them both [Archie Randolph Ammons and John Ashbery] as poets and persons, yet I was closer to Archie and more in awe of John. Both were major poets and central to American tradition. Now, in early January 2018, I realize that the Age of Ashbery has just ended, even as the [Wallace] Stevens era reached conclusion in early August 1955, a month before I started my ongoing teaching career at Yale.

The body of these chapters devoted to his friends and acquaintances is generally a close reading of a poem or two that Bloom has memorized and now finds himself chanting or reciting during his late-life bouts with insomnia. Most also include some type of reference to their position in Bloom's taxonomy of literary greatness.

It is hard not to read this volume and feel the pain of loss both in the often profoundly poignant poetry and prose Bloom cites as well as in occasional comments like:

> At seventy-two I had experienced many losses, but at eighty-seven I feel abandoned by virtually everyone I loved in my own generation. They are all gone, perhaps into a world of light, or a final darkness. In the last month, a great poet and a magnificent critic have departed, both of them friends for more than sixty years.

Bloom comments in his "Preface" that the book "is not intended to be a lamentation for my own generation of critics and poets," but rather "a living tribute to their afterlife in their writings." The "friends" include "John Ashbery, A. R. Ammons, Mark Strand, Alvin Feinman, Richard Rorty, Geoffrey Hartman, Angus Fletcher, and John Hollander"; the "mentors" include M. H. Abrams, Frederick Pottle, Gershom Scholem, Hans Joas, and Kenneth Burke; and the acquaintances include "Frank Kermode, Anthony Burgess, A. D. Nuttall, Northrop Frye." There are of course many others who receive "living tribute" in the volume including former students, and many other contemporary poets and critics who were either friends or acquaintances such as Richard Eberhart, Weldon Kees, May Swenson, and John Wheelwright.

I agree with Bloom that the book is not a "lamentation" to his friends and mentors, and also agree that it is a form of "living tribute." However, it is difficult not to conclude after reading five-hundred pages of reflection on writers and writing ranging from the poetry of Kabbalah and Psalms to Jay Macpherson and Amy Clampitt that this book is more a living tribute to "great" literature and its major characters than to Bloom's friends, acquaintances, and mentors. The energy and passion for literature in this volume is always backward looking, and never forward looking. Bloom announces, for example, that the ages of Wallace and Ashbery have ended, whereas clearly the age of Kabbalah and Shakespeare cannot ever end. The "living" tributaries are given short commentaries whereas literary giants like Shakespeare and Whitman are dealt with in great detail and energy.

At the close of Part Two, which is devoted to readings of his favorite texts and characters from Shakespeare, Bloom is clear about how literature ends: namely, when its bewilderment ceases *for him*:

> I must have been nine or ten when I first read Shakespeare. I went from *Julius Caesar*; which I almost understood, on to *Hamlet*, where I was both fascinated and baffled. *Hamlet* still changes for me each time I return to it. How can you come to the end of it? Dante's *Paradiso* still defeats me. Old age has not reconciled me to it. I am a Jew who evades normative Judaism. My religion is the appreciation of high literature. Shakespeare is the summit. Revelation for me is Shakespeare or nothing.

Oddly, in spite of his exalted status as high literature, we hear very little about Dante in this book aside from a passing comment or so. This is even more apparent when compared to his extensive readings of the Hebrew Bible, Shakespeare, or even Whitman.

What becomes obvious then about this book is that it is *not* celebrating the highest literature in the Western tradition. If so, because of the exalted place of Dante as high literature, there would at least be a chapter among the seventy-five in the book devoted to him. It is also *not* really a living tribute to his friends and acquaintances, as there are only sixteen chapters devoted to folks that fit this description. However, if we don't count the three chapters on Wallace Stevens, whom he only met once as a nineteen-year-old after a talk at Yale, this leaves thirteen chapters of seventy-five devoted by title to living tributes to people Bloom knew in the flesh: Angus Fletcher, A. R. Ammons, Conrad Aiken, Richard Eberhart, Weldon Kees, May Swenson, Delmore Schwartz, Alvin Feinman, John Ashbery, John Wheelwright, James Merrill, Jay Macpherson, and Amy Clampitt. While it is true that he mentions and discusses many others especially Frederick Pottle and Gershom Scholem, their tribute is always secondary to the text or author at the center of the chapter. To whom then is this volume a living tribute? In short, the answer is: Bloom.

111

Possessed by Memory is a tribute to Bloom's lifetime in search of revelation through literature. As a type of secular rabbi, the religion of literature has taken him on an inward journey through readings of the words of others to a discovery of his own humanity. As the end-of-life approaches, he is taking stock of this journey through the words and characters that have been writ upon his memory. Throughout the book he alternately chants, recites, teaches, and thinks about these works. He truly is "possessed" by this literature writ upon his memory as it often appears to act uncontrollably in and on his life, "filling him with the blessing of more life." This book is in effect a record of this possession and his effort to take stock of a life defined by it. Also, it is an effort to assess the literature and characters possessed by his memory with respect to their place in his hierarchy of literary greatness.

In sum, *Possessed by Memory* is Bloom's autobiography: the record of his soul. He points this out to us in a quote from Oscar Wilde's "The Critic as Artist" (1891), which is the epigraph to the book.

> That is what the highest criticism really is, the record of one's own soul. It is more fascinating than history, as it is concerned simply with oneself. It is more delightful than philosophy, as its subject is concrete and not abstract, real not vague. It is the only civilized form of autobiography, as it deals not with events, but with the thoughts of one's life; not with life's physical accidents of deed or circumstance, but with the spiritual moods and imaginative passions of the mind.

But if this book is indeed "the highest criticism," a form of criticism with intellectual roots in Dr. Samuel Johnson, who "has been [Bloom's] model," as well as William Hazlitt, John Ruskin, Walter Pater, Oscar Wilde, Ralph Waldo Emerson, William James, and Kenneth Burke, and a literary art critical tradition that Bloom has made a "conscious effort to follow," it is also a form of criticism that feels dated today— one that will end with the passing of Bloom just like the ages of Stevens and Ashbery came to an end with their passing. This is particularly apparent when this type of influence criticism is placed in the context of the cornucopia of contemporary literary and cultural theory that has developed since Bloom famously "broke with [Northrop] Frye, not personally but intellectually, in the summer of 1967, when [he] first drafted what was to become *The Anxiety of Influence* [1973]."

Aside from a couple of passing remarks about the state of our nation and world today (e.g., "Because of American politics, and our crusading zeal abroad, one needs to keep the Bible apart from the way we live now") and an occasional comment on the sexuality of a writer ("[May Swenson] realized early that her sexual orientation was lesbian"), it reveals literature to have no connection with critical citizenship or democratic values let alone our current critical commonplaces such as race, class, gender, and sexuality in their full intersectional complexity.

Bloom amply demonstrates that high literature can be a religion that brings richness to individual lives, but only at the cost of turning its back on the problems of society and the world. Bloom's religion of high literature with its hierarchies of aesthetic greatness served the critical climate of his generation well. But as his generation fades away, so too must this form of criticism if it is unable to provide direction regarding the challenges facing our technologically and militarily advanced albeit increasing religiously divided world.

A REPLY FROM HAROLD BLOOM

I regret that I have never encountered Jeffrey R. Di Leo. His review is gracious and his social concern is commendable. That said, I totally dissent from his conclusion. It would not be literary criticism in the Johnsonian sense when he calls for a discourse to ameliorate our Trump-infested and deeply hurt nation. We have much more than enough amateur sociology, anthropology, political science, and passionately committed resentment. We do not need it from the literary critic. Her function is to appreciate the cognitive power, originality, and beauty of the highest literature.[5]

113

14 | DON'T SHOOT THE JOURNAL EDITOR

Academic publishing can be a rough place.

Recently, threats of personal violence against a journal editor for publishing a controversial essay were widely reported.

The editor's concerned publisher looked into the threats and found them to be both "serious" and "credible."

"So, you're really going to break my editor's thumbs if we don't withdraw the essay?" you could imagine the publisher asking.

"Just try me," the snarling thug might reply. "You've got 24 hours to make that essay go away or we *start* with the thumbs!"

After the essay received 16,000 online views in just a couple of weeks, the publisher succumbed to the threats and withdrew the essay from the journal. Today, in place of an essay, one finds the following:

WITHDRAWAL NOTICE

This Viewpoint essay has been withdrawn at the request of the academic journal editor, and in agreement with the author of the essay. Following a number of complaints, Taylor & Francis conducted a thorough investigation into the peer review process on this article. Whilst this clearly demonstrated the essay had undergone double-blind peer review, in line with the journal's editorial policy, the journal editor has subsequently received serious and credible threats of personal violence. These threats are linked to the publication of this essay. As the publisher, we must take this seriously. Taylor & Francis has a strong and supportive duty of care to all our academic editorial teams, and this is why we are withdrawing this essay.

And, to be perfectly accurate, the threats of violence were not directed at the thumbs of the journal editor. Rather, they were against his life.

The journal editor called the author of the essay and said, "We're getting death threats. Do you mind if we withdrew it?" The author agreed, and the essay was withdrawn with his consent.

The editor, Shahid Qadir, received a piece from Bruce Gilley, a professor of political science at Portland State University. The journal, *Third World Quarterly* (*TWQ*), founded in 1979, and edited by Qadir since 1990, had already published two peer-reviewed articles by Gilley, so he was no stranger to them.

The article, "The Case for Colonialism," was submitted by Gilley to a special issue of the journal on the new imperialism. The editors of the special issue quickly rejected the article as not suitable for it.

In recounting this process, Gilley says,

> Obviously [my article] wasn't suitable for their special issue because their special issue was going to be a critique of what they considered the latest round of imperialism. My article did not share their ideological slant. It was therefore, ipso facto, not appropriate for their special issue. That was a desk rejection, not a peer-review rejection.

But this was not the first time that the article was rejected. It was submitted to another journal, whose editor regarded it as "a very powerful piece," and proposed to his board that it be published along with critical responses—in spite of two peer reviews that concluded that it should be rejected. Wisely, the editorial board "anticipated a fury" and decided that publishing it with responses "was not worth the grief."

So, by the time Gilley submitted it to another journal for publication, he was surely well aware that it would be regarded as a controversial piece. In fact, as he says above, he knew that it "Obviously was not suitable" for the special issue of *TWQ*.

Thus, one might ask Gilley, why then he submitted an article to the journal that he knew was not suitable to its special issue?

It is one thing to not know that it is suitable, and to find it out later. It is entirely another thing to know in advance it is not suitable, but to send it anyway. The former one can accept on the grounds of naiveté; the latter though might be regarded as irresponsible, if not also, a species of unprofessional behavior. If you know something is not suitable or acceptable, but submit it anyway, you are arguably just wasting your time, the time of others, and the valuable but limited resources of the journal.

It is no secret that many journals have ideological slants. Sending them work that goes against these slants is to ask for rejection. But maybe this is all Gilley really wanted in the first place? Namely, for *TWQ* to just reject his article. For some authors, this form of rejection is a real badge of honor—and for others, it is even a form of academic thrill.

Desk rejection is part of the peer review process—and not something distinct from it as Gilley suggests in his comment above. Submissions that are not suitable for a journal will often be rejected without enlisting the efforts of additional peers. For example, a short story submitted to a journal that publishes literary criticism does not get further than the desk of the journal editor. And, a work of continental philosophy is not sent out for peer review when submitted to an analytic philosophy journal.

As a journal editor, I'm not in favor of people sending submissions that they know will be rejected—though over the years I have seen my share of them. In fact, some folks make a career out of doing this kind of thing. Also, splitting the peer review hair into "desk" and "non-desk" peer review to explain away a rejection that was expected all along seems silly to me.

But what Qadir did after *TWQ*'s "desk rejection" is not only a bit unexpected, but also admirable. It reveals the value he places as an editor on ensuring that the journal he oversees is "a forum for informed and reasoned debate"—one of its foundational principles—and not just doctrinaire dismissal of reasoned counter-statement.

It is also the action that led to death threats against him.

Instead of using the rejection of his special issue editors as an opportunity to be done with Gilley's submission, Qadir thought that it should be considered for a general submission to the journal (albeit one that would surely attract debate). Two reviews of the submission were then sought: one came back positive and the other negative.

Qadir then decided to publish Gilley's submission as a "viewpoint essay"—rather than quash discussion of his "controversial" position on colonialism.

Soon after Gilley's viewpoint essay appeared in the journal, a petition was circulated to "retract" the article from the journal. It quickly gathered more than *ten thousand* signatures.

In addition, fifteen members of its thirty-four member editorial board resigned over the "process" that led to the publication of the essay. At least one member of the editorial board though did not: Noam Chomsky.

He dissented from the mass resignation, saying "Journals often don't follow proper procedure." "In such a case," commented Chomsky, "the editor should explain and apologize publicly, as I assume [Qadir] will." "I don't think that's a sufficient reason to destroy a journal—the likely consequence of mass resignation."

Also, in opposition to the calls from the resigning board members that the article be "retracted," Chomsky said that publishing a rebuttal to the essay would be an educational opportunity for its readership.

Gilley responded to Chomsky's support for not retracting the essay (against the chorus of calls for its retraction) by only further fanning the flames of controversy by saying that the internationally famous public intellectual's support is an example of the "well-known schism between the old left and the new left." "Noam Chomsky is a member of the old left," comments Gilley, "and the old left was fully conversant in the importance of debate and dialectic." "It's the new left, the cultural left, the safe-spaces left, that is where the schism is."

In their resignation letter, the Editorial Board members said, "We all subscribe to the principle of freedom of speech and the value of provocation in order to generate critical debate." "However, this cannot be done by means of a piece that fails to meet academic standards of rigour [sic] and balance by ignoring all manner of violence, exploitation and harm perpetrated in the name of colonialism (and imperialism) and that causes offence [sic] and hurt and thereby clearly violates that very principle of free speech."

Also, in the wake of these events, his university issued a written statement saying that it affirms "the right of all our faculty to explore scholarship and to speak, write, and publish a variety of viewpoints and conclusions." It also added, that it "does not endorse the viewpoint of Professor Gilley's article."

Students at his university also filed a harassment claim against him. Reports Gilley, they are "claiming that I'm engaging in prohibited harassment and discrimination." "So for the last four months I've been subject to a wide-ranging investigation by our diversity office." And he added, "I have an attorney now."

Since the death threats to the journal editor and "withdrawal" of the essay from *TWQ* in 2017, a colloquium on the essay was held on May 7, 2018 at The McDonald Centre for Theology, Ethics & Public Life" at Oxford University. A notice for the colloquium at Oxford says that the "furore" over the essay was "predictable," and that the purpose of the event is "to examine Gilley's reading of the colonial past; to test his proposals for a 'neo-colonial' future; and to reflect on the controversy." In addition to Gilley, thirty historians, economists, ethicists, experts in international relations, and former civil servants attended the event.

The following month, the essay was re-published by the National Association of Scholars (NAS). Their quarterly journal, *Academic Questions*, did so "to ensure that it will be permanently available to students, scholars, and the general public."

NAS also determined that a few weeks before Gilley's "viewpoint" essay was published in *TWQ*, another was published without *any* double-blind peer review—namely, that of Vijay Prashad, an Editorial Board member and one of the most outspoken critics of the publication "process" for Gilley's essay.

In their press release about the re-publication, NAS President Peter Wood said "The efforts to censor Bruce Gilley's article and the attacks on him personally were outrageous." "Gilley published a well-reasoned and humane perspective on the political and economic challenges that face many Third World nations. Anyone who actually reads the article will see his thoughtful tone and good will." "But we live in a time when many in the academic world believe they have the right to prevent the expression of views they disagree with," continues Wood. "The actions of those who sought to suppress Gilley's article demonstrate this. The intolerance and anti-intellectualism displayed in this instance reached a new extreme."

NAS additionally reported that Gilley too received death threats.

Discussion of this essay and its publication process has been widespread. Gilley and others have done many interviews about it, and there are also a number of articles and blog discussions concerning the topic. Moreover, there does not seem to be an end in sight. In fact, later this fall,[6] Gilley is scheduled to give a talk at The Institute for the

Study of Western Civilization at Texas Tech University. Its title is "The Case for Colonialism."

While I admire Qadir's editorial courage in going forward with the publication of this article, I do think that given its *prima facie* "controversial" position, he should have pursued the route of the first editor who reviewed it, and opted to publish it with responses. Respondents might have included critics such as Hamid Dabashi, the Hagop Kevorkian Professor of Iranian Studies and Comparative Literature at Columbia University, who wrote an essay for the Al-Jazeera website on the publication controversy entitled "Moral Paralysis in American Academia."

Dabashi's take on Chomsky's call for rebuttal rather than retraction of the essay is that Chomsky "has as usual refused to denounce Bruce Gilley, offering his habitual bourgeois hogwash that a professor has the right to say what he said and that he too publishes things that offend people. This, of course, is highbrow gibberish— shifting the issue to the domain of censorship and freedom of speech."

Dabashi writes that Gilley "must be ostracized, publicly shamed and humiliated, and never ever called a 'colleague' who should be politely invited for a 'civilized debate.' Against that 'civilized' gathering of morally compromised scholars, I will proudly form a band of barbarian dissidents."

Following Columbia professor Dabashi's logic here, both Oxford University and Texas Tech University must also be "must be ostracized, publicly shamed and humiliated" for their efforts at civilized debate on Gilley's essay.

Journals that provide "a forum for informed and reasoned debate" need to be supported in the publication of both non-controversial *and* controversial topics. And editors like Shahid Qadir who value this type of debate are to be championed—not scorned. I guess in a day and age when politicians regularly and publicly ostracize, shame, and humiliate their opponents, it is understandable why professors like Dabashi might think this is ok. But once academics give up the high ground of critical debate as the modus operandi of higher education— and descend into bullying, mob mentality, and death threats to forward their positions—there is really is no need for journals or journal editors that facilitate informed and reasoned debate.

The *TWQ* affair is not just about how to handle controversial material in a journal, but raises questions about the future of encouraging and facilitating reasoned debate in academic journals. And even though the thousands of retractors got their wish, and the essay is no longer available in *TWQ*, so too did the proponents of censorship, bullying, and intimidation. In the process of opposing a controversial and objectionable position, scholars have lowered themselves to the level of the bullies and thugs they aim to oppose and rise above.

121

15 | DOES PHILOSOPHY NEED A STORY?

In May of 1923, the publisher Emanuel Haldeman-Julius heard that the philosopher Will Durant would be in Kansas City, so decided to drive there from his home in Girard, Kansas to meet up with him. Haldeman-Julius first met Durant during World War I. Durant, who completed his doctorate in philosophy at Columbia University in 1917, published his first book the same year. Entitled *Philosophy and the Social Problem*, Durant argued that philosophy had not grown because it avoided the actual problems of society.

Haldeman-Julius liked Durant's non-technical approach to philosophy, and Durant in turn liked Haldeman-Julius's ideas. So, Haldeman-Julius traveled to Kansas City intent on signing the philosopher to write for the *Haldeman-Julius Weekly*. It was a progressive newspaper he had just launched on December 9, 1922 with a blistering attack on the Ku Klux Klan, which he described as "something slimy which had crept out of the gutter. It represents organized hatred, bigotry, maliciousness, jealousy, and cruelty. It is living proof that America is not a civilized country."

Haldeman-Julius prevailed, and Durant went on for the next three years to write a series of essays on philosophy for the progressive publisher located in America's heartland. These essays were published by Haldeman-Julius as "Little Blue Books," a series of little (3½ inches by 5 inches), short (32 to 64 pages) books printed on inexpensive paper that sold for as little as 5 or 10 cents. The series, launched in 1919, found in Durant, an author that sold surprisingly well: as of 1928, Durant's Little Blue Book on the philosophy of Henri Bergson had sold 8,000 copies; Herbert Spencer, 19,000 copies; Voltaire, 24,000; Immanuel Kant, 24,000; Francis Bacon, 25,500; Arthur Schopenhauer, 26,500; Aristotle, 27,000, and Plato, 39,000. The best-selling one though was his essay on Nietzsche, which as of 1928, had sold 45,000 copies.

In July of 1925, Haldeman-Julius was in New York City for a vacation with his wife, Marcet. While there he met with M. Lincoln Schuster of the publishing house, Simon and Schuster. Like Haldeman-

Julius, who became notorious and successful for publishing books on topics such as sex, birth control, prostitution, and freethinking, Schuster too gained notoriety and success in the early 1920s albeit for taking advantage of the country's crossword puzzle craze by founding a company in 1924 with Richard Simon to publish them.

Over lunch, Schuster told Haldeman-Julius that unlike the publisher of the Little Blue Books, he was not interested in the mass production of books. Rather, Schuster just wanted to produce a few quality books, and picked Haldeman-Julius's brain for book ideas. "How about a good, well-written history of philosophy," suggested Haldeman-Julius. "But who would write it?" asked Schuster. "There are not many Will Durants," responded Haldeman-Julius.

The more he thought about Schuster's question the more he became convinced that Will Durant should be the author. So he pitched the idea of publishing Durant's fifteen Little Blue Books on philosophy in one volume. Schuster thought this was a good idea, and a year later, *The Story of Philosophy: The Lives and Opinions of the Greater Philosophers* (1926) came out.

It proved to be both a ground-breaking and best-selling book that made Durant financially independent. This allowed him to leave teaching to focus on writing the eleven-volume work, *The Story of Civilization* (1935-1975), of which the first six volumes would carry only his name, while the final five would carry the name of his wife, Ariel, as co-author. The writing on this multivolume project would go on for the next four decades. The tenth volume, *Rousseau and Revolution* (1967), was awarded the Pulitzer Prize for General Nonfiction, and the Durants received the Presidential Medal of Freedom in 1977 from U.S. President Gerald Ford for their work on the multivolume series.

Durant later expressed his appreciation to Haldeman-Julius, writing to him "I owe you two great debts: first, you took the initial chance on me and had the unprecedented courage of putting philosophy into a magazine and into your booklets and second that you secured Simon and Schuster as publishers." Moreover, if Haldeman-Julius had not introduced Durant to Schuster, who knows if either of these beloved "stories" would have ever been published: one that helped to popularize philosophy in the United States, and the other that became the most successful historiographical series in history—and put Simon & Schuster on the publishing map. But neither "story" is without its critics and controversies. And Durant was well aware of this from the beginning.

He entitled both of these projects "stories" to differentiate them from the work published by specialists in philosophy and history. In his opening address, "To the Reader," in the 1926 edition of *The Story of Philosophy*, Durant acknowledges the idiosyncratic nature of his project: "This book is not a complete history of philosophy. It is an attempt to humanize knowledge by centering the story of speculative thought around certain dominant personalities." The philosophers he focuses on are Plato, Aristotle, Bacon, Spinoza, Voltaire, Kant, Schopenhauer, Spencer, Nietzsche, Bergson, Croce, Russell, Santayana, James, and Dewey—albeit the latter six in much less detail than the others. He continues:

> Certain lesser figures have been omitted in order that those selected might have the space required to make them live. Hence the inadequate treatment of the half-legendary pre-Socratics, the Stoics and Epicureans, the Scholastics, and the epistemologists. The author believes that epistemology has kidnapped modern philosophy, and well-nigh ruined it; he hopes for the time when the study of the knowledge-process will be recognized as the business of the science of psychology, and when philosophy will again be understood as the synthetic interpretation of all experience rather than the analytic description of the mode and process of experience itself.

Moreover, he continues his assault on analytic and professional philosophy by refusing to acknowledge the importance of the "parts of philosophy" to its study. For him the practice of philosophy as logic, aesthetics, ethics, social and political philosophy, and metaphysics (which includes ontology, philosophical psychology, and epistemology) "dismembered it" and led it to lose "its beauty and its joy." "We shall seek it," continues Durant, "not in its shrivelled [sic] abstractness and formality, but clothed in the living form of genius; we shall study not merely philosophies, but philosophers; we shall spend our time with the saints and martyrs of thought, letting their

125

radiant spirit play about us until perhaps we too, in some measure, shall partake of what Leonardo called 'the noblest pleasure, the joy of understanding.'"

When I first encountered Durant's "story" about philosophy, it was as someone who had never taken a college course in philosophy but had read works from a number of the philosophers discussed in his book. His style of writing was engaging and his outlines of the opinions of these philosophers were clear and easy to understand. So aside from the sin of omission, what was not to like about it?

Over the years, as I came to take more and more university courses in philosophy, both as an undergraduate and a graduate student, Durant's "story" became an increasingly inadequate one. I cannot recall any of my philosophy professors at any level speaking well of this book. In fact, I learned that it is best to dismiss it as mere "popular" philosophy that pales compared to the work of specialists in the various areas of philosophy.

A few months ago, a friend of mine, who had just "discovered" Durant's book, shared his excitement about it to me and asked me my opinion of it. While I gave him the obligatory professional philosopher dismissal of it, I found myself dissatisfied with the response. It was not that the book had changed in terms of its content (the version found in every Barnes & Noble philosophy section in America is still basically the same text as found in the first edition and the Little Blue Books). But rather it was that the market for "popular" philosophy has changed.

Whereas in 1926, philosophy in America had not yet become "popularized," today it is. Academic and trade publishers alike now have many options available for learning about philosophy short of plowing through primary philosophical writings. They include a wide variety of dictionaries, handbooks, glossaries, textbooks, and anthologies. Major philosophy publishers like Oxford University Press and Routledge now even put out book series of "very short" introductions to major philosophers and ideas in philosophy, some of which like Peter Singer's *Hegel: A Very Short Introduction* (Oxford, 2001) are written by major contemporary philosophers.

There are also a variety of "illustrated" introductions to philosophy such as *Introducing Hegel—A Graphic Guide* (Icon Books, 2012) written by Lloyd Spenser and illustrated by Andrzej Krauze, a book that was formally published under the title, *Hegel for Beginners* (Icon Books, 1992). Think too of books like *Star Trek and Philosophy* (Open Court, 2008) where twenty-one professional philosophers address philosophical issues in the television and movie series. There is even another book called *The Story of Philosophy* that is now in its second edition (DK, 2016) written by Bryan Magee who has taught philosophy at Oxford University (though even today, it does not sell as well as Durant's original). The list here is endless. And many of these books like the ones above are written by professional philosophers— folks from the same group that today still sneers at Durant's "story."

Given the plethora of options for "popular" philosophy today, it seems untimely to dismiss summarily Durant's story—even if one is a professional philosopher. Why? Because to take it down is also to take down the immense market for and range of popular philosophy books today. Many of which, like my own book, *From Socrates to Cinema* (McGraw-Hill, 2007), are aimed at college students and general readers who are interested in philosophy but find many of its primary texts too daunting and much of its contemporary professional writing completely inaccessible. In *From Socrates to Cinema*, I address this challenge directly by using both short stories and films in conjunction with more traditional philosophical writing, to introduce the reader to philosophy.

In 1953, over twenty-five years after the publication of the first edition of *The Story of Philosophy*, the 68 year old Durant was asked by his publishers to write a new preface to the second edition. Taking his title from John Henry Newman's famous defense of his religious opinions, *Apologia Pro Vita Sua (Defense of One's Own Life*, 1864), Durant defended his philosophical opinions with the tongue-in-cheek title, "Apologia Pro Libro Suo," which literally means "a defense of one's own book."

He begins by reminding us that in the first quarter of the twentieth-century, "outlines" like his were all the rage. "Human knowledge had become unmanageably vast; every science had begotten a dozen more, each subtler than the rest," and "millions of voices called for" help from writers and publishers to navigate it. Durant ridicules "specialists" in science and philosophy saying "the scientific specialist [was one] who knew 'more and more about less and less,' and the philosophical speculator [was one] who knew less

127

and less about more and more." "The specialist," snarks Durant, "put on blinders in order to shut out from his vision all the world but one little spot, to which he glued his nose."

Much like today, where understanding science and philosophy involves mastery of a discipline specific vocabulary, Durant bemoaned that in the mid-1920s, "Every science, and every branch of philosophy, developed a technical terminology intelligible only to its exclusive devotees." He saw a situation in science and philosophy where people educated in these areas "found themselves ever less capable of expressing to their educated fellow-men what it was that they had learned."

For Durant, the problem with this communication gap between specialists and non-specialists is a political one. Without teachers to bridge this gap, he feared a rise of authoritarianism. Writes Durant, "if knowledge became too great for communication, it would degenerate into scholasticism, and the weak acceptance of authority; mankind would slip into a new age of faith, worshipping at a respectful distance its new priests; and civilization, which had hoped to raise itself upon education disseminated far and wide, would be left precariously based upon technical erudition that had become the monopoly of an esoteric class monastically isolated from the world by the high birth rate of terminology."

In a way, his project in *The Story of Philosophy* is much like the one H. G. Wells set out to achieve in *The Outline of History* (1919-1920), which was written to educate the masses about history in order to avoid "catastrophe"—or more simply put, to save the world. Also, Durant rightly sees his own book as comparable to Wells's book, which he says was criticized for its "errors" and which historians "did not quite know what to do with." "History became popular" with the publication of *The Outline of History* writes Durant, "and historians became alarmed." "Now it would be necessary for them to write as interestingly as H. G. Wells."

Durant points out that his book was written at a time when there was a "flood" of "story" and "outline" books: "Outline followed outline, 'story' followed 'story'; science and art, religion and law, had their storiographers." But the market for these "story" and "outline" books was soon saturated, and the public appetite was quickly satiated; critics and professors complained of superficiality and haste, and an undertow of resentment set in, which reached every outline [and story] from the last to the first. As quickly as it had come, the fashion changed; no one dared any longer say a word for the humanization of knowledge; the denunciation of outlines was now the easy road to critical repute; it became the style to speak with a delicate superiority of any non-fiction book that could be understood. The snob movement in literature began.

Twenty-five years after the publication of his book, Durant does not shy away from the conditions of its production, nor does he deny that many of the criticisms of it are warranted. "The worst sin of all—though the critics do not seem to have noticed it—was the omission of Chinese and Hindu philosophy." "Even a 'story' of philosophy that begins with Socrates, and has nothing to say about Lao-tze and Confucius, Mencius and Chwang-tze, Buddha and Shankara, is provincially incomplete," he continues. He claims that his attempt to atone for the omission of Eastern philosophy was the publication in 1935 of *Our Oriental Heritage*, the first volume of his *The Story of Civilization*.

"As for the word 'Story,' which has since been so abused with use, it was chosen partly to indicate that the record would concern itself chiefly with the more vital philosophers, partly to convey the sense that the development of thought was a romance as stirring as any in history." But in spite of all its flaws, the book allegedly raised interest in the philosophical classics. According to Durant, "sales of the philosophical classics increased some two hundred per cent. [sic] after the publication of the *Story*." He continues:

> Many publishers have issued new editions, particularly of Plato, Spinoza, Voltaire, Schopenhauer and Nietzsche. A high official of the New York Public Library, who asked to be unnamed, reports that: ever since the publication of *The Story of Philosophy* we have had a wide and increasing demand from the public for the philosophical classics, and our stock of them in branch libraries has been gradually increased . . . Formally, current books about philosophy were purchased in small quantities

129

for the system; but in the last two or three years a readable new book about philosophy is purchased very generally at the outset, in anticipation of a demand which eventually does develop, and quickly at that.

Durant adds too that as of 1953, the book was already translated into German, French, Swedish, Danish, Jugo-Slavian, Chinese, Japanese and Hungarian. Today, many other languages have been added to the list, and it still has a global readership. One can easily find, for example, online comments about it from enthusiastic lay readers from across the world in Arabic, Chinese, Russian, and a host of other languages.

Durant reminds us that we should not be "ashamed of teaching the people" even if we are "imperfect" at it by some standards. "We are all imperfect teachers, but we may be forgiven if we have advanced the matter a little, and have done our best." He did his best spending eleven years researching the material in his book, and three years writing it first as series of Little Blue Books aimed at lay readers, and then publishing it as one volume at the request of M. Lincoln Schuster.

Today, close to one-hundred years after Durant offered us a "story" about philosophy complete with humor and colorful characters, the book continues to be widely read by non-specialists— and disparaged by specialists. However, the story of philosophy today does not end with John Dewey, and if anything, philosophy has become even more specialized and complex over the past century. But the world today is not unlike the world of Wells and Durant in that it flirts daily with "catastrophe" and has seen a rise in authoritarianism. Educated opinion seems to be in short supply, and the world stage is now open to bullies, tyrants and dictators. In addition, in spite of the plethora of popular options to learn about philosophy, its popularity seems to be waning. Philosophy departments are being closed and the major struggles to attract students compared to vocational ones such as business, nursing, and engineering.

Philosophy needs a "story" now more than ever. Durant's "enduring" "romance" served its audience well, but it is time for a new one—a story that transitions philosophy from the twentieth century to the twenty-first, and not the nineteenth century to the twentieth like the original. Why not hope too that it is a "story" or a series of "short stories" that saves academic philosophy from obsolescence in the age of authoritarianism and vocational training? This would be an ironic and bittersweet victory for Durant after a century of dismissal of his own "story" by academic philosophers.

16 | MUSIC CONTRA LIFE

Music like literature and the other arts plays an important role in life. For many, it is a source of entertainment, enjoyment, and pleasure. For others though such as the late Miles Davis, its role in their lives is much greater: something closer to a life-giving force, rather than merely a pleasant diversion. One has an intimation of this power when the musician summed up his life with the statement, "Music has been my life"—a statement wherein one feels both the potential of music to *give* life as well as to *take it away*.

Still, in spite of the power of music over life, almost nothing has been written about it in the philosophical tradition. The most significant comments on the topic come from Friedrich Nietzsche, particularly in 1888, the last (and most) productive year of his life, a year in which he wrote five books: *The Case of Wagner, The Antichrist, Ecce Homo, Nietzsche contra Wagner,* and *Twilight of the Idols*, the book where he made the famous comment, "Without music, life would be an error."

But Nietzsche's thoughts on the relationship between music and life go much deeper than just this line now featured on t-shirts. In the fall of 1888, the philosopher stayed in Turin, Italy. During his stay, he went through his older writing going back as far as 1877 and selected pieces that reflected his position on the composer, Richard Wagner. The pieces, often shortened and clarified, were to become his final book, *Nietzsche contra Wagner*—a book that would not be published until many years later, that is, in 1895 in volume eight of his collected works.

Nietzsche wrote the preface for *Nietzsche contra Wagner* on Christmas of 1888 and then early the next month he became insane, after which, his friend and former colleague, Franz Overbeck, transported him back to Basel, Switzerland from Turin. He was then committed to the asylum in Jena, Germany, but shortly thereafter released to the care of his mother in Naumburg, Germany. When his mother died in 1897, his sister moved him to Weimar, Germany, where he died on August 25, 1900.

Nietzsche contra Wagner leaves little doubt about his position on the composer. "We are antipodes," writes Nietzsche in the preface, a position that he contends will not be a popular one with German readers. "I have readers everywhere," says Nietzsche, "in Vienna, in St. Petersburg, in Copenhagen and Stockholm, in Paris, in New York—I do *not* have them in Europe's shallows, Germany."

His critique of the music of Wagner in this work and others is interesting both for what it is (a "physiological" one) and for what it is not (an "aesthetic" one). In fact, in the preface he alludes to this by saying that the book is "an essay for psychologists, but *not* for Germans." Though Nietzsche "admire[s] Wagner wherever he puts himself into music," "[t]his does not mean that I consider this music healthy." In brief, Nietzsche contends that the music of Wagner is not only *unhealthy*, but also that the composer himself is a "sickness."

In *The Case of Wagner*, published in September of 1888, and the last book that Nietzsche would see to publication before his breakdown, he is direct and clear about the effect of Wagner and his music on our health:

> I am far from looking on guilelessly while this decadent corrupts our health—and music as well. Is Wagner a human being at all? Isn't he rather a sickness? He makes sick whatever he touches—*he has made music sick—*

Later, in the same section of *The Case of Wagner*, Nietzsche reflects further on the relationship between sickness, health, and life:

> To sense that what is harmful is harmful, to be *able* to forbid oneself something harmful, is a sign of youth and vitality. The exhausted are *attracted* by what is harmful: the vegetarian by vegetables. Sickness itself can be a stimulant to life: one only has to be healthy enough for the stimulant.

Health for Nietzsche involves a certain type of resilience, one that allows some people to "instinctively cho[ose] the *right* means against wretched states." It is the resiliency of the healthy person that enables them to use sickness as a "stimulant to life." A variant of this line written in the same year (1888) from *Ecce Homo* links this all back to the development of a philosophy:

A typically healthy person, conversely, being sick can even become an energetic *stimulus* for life, for living *more*. This, in fact, is how that long period of sickness appears to me *now*: as it were, I discovered life anew, including myself; I tasted all good and even little things, as others cannot easily taste them—I turned my will to health, to *life*, into a philosophy.

The significance of these passages stems less with the German philosopher's specific problems with the music of Wagner or, for that matter, with vegetarianism (Wagner was a vegetarian and Hitler is claimed to have followed the composer's dietary practice), but rather with the way in which what we now call "biopolitics" enters into a dialogue with music through the late writing of Nietzsche.

Michel Foucault first introduced the problematic of biopower in his lectures at the Collège de France in the spring of 1976, and then devoted his next two years of lectures at the Collège to developing his thoughts on biopolitics. In his final lecture in 1976 under the course title "Society Must Be Defended," he notes that in the second half of the eighteenth century "a new technology of power" emerges. He terms it here "biopower" and "biopolitics."

Foucault explains that while biopower "does not exclude disciplinary technology...it does dovetail into it, integrate it, modify it to some extent, and above all, use it by sort of infiltrating it, embedding itself in existing disciplinary techniques." "Unlike discipline, which is addressed to bodies," biopower "is applied not to man-as-body but to the living man, to man-as-living-being; ultimately, if you like, to man-as-species." Biopower addresses "man-as-species" as "a global mass that is affected by overall processes characteristic of birth, death, production, illness, and so on." It is a "seizure of power that is not individualizing but, if you like, massifying, that is directed not at man-as-body but at man-as-species."

The first object of biopolitics are processes "such as the ration of births to deaths, the rate of reproduction, the fertility of the population, and so on." In the second half of the eighteenth century, biopolitics seeks to control these processes. It is here that "the first demographers begin to measure these phenomena in statistical terms." During this period, death is "no longer something that suddenly swooped down on life—as in an epidemic." Death becomes "permanent, something that slips into life, perpetually gnaws at it, diminishes it and weakens it."

While Foucault enumerates many different elements that enter into the domain of biopolitics both in its early stages and its later stages, he says "biopolitics will derive its knowledge from, and define its power's field of intervention in terms of, the birth rate, the morality rate, various biological disabilities, and the effects of the environment." Also, in addition, it "deals with the population, with the population as a political problem, as a problem that is at once scientific and political, as a biological problem and as power's problem." Biopolitics is as well credited by Foucault with introducing "forecasts, statistical estimates, and overall measures."

The topic of "bio-politics" is also discussed by Foucault around the same time in *The History of Sexuality: Volume 1* (1978). In the section of this book entitled "Right of Death and Power over Life," Foucault discusses "the ancient right to *take* life or *let* live" that comes to be replaced beginning in the eighteenth-century by "a power to *foster* life or *disallow* it to the point of death." The context here is the change in the right of the sovereign to take life through the death penalty. Focus in the application of capital punishment shifts from emphasizing the "enormity of the crime" to "the safeguard of society" and "the monstrosity of the criminal." "Now it is over life, throughout its unfolding," comments Foucault, "that power establishes its dominion; death is power's limit, the moment that escapes it; death becomes the most secret aspect of existence, the most 'private.'"

Under the aegis of an emerging biopolitics, "life more than the law . . . became the issue of political struggles" to the point where even Aristotle's observations on the nature of man as a political animal were no longer valid. Whereas "[f]or millennia, man remained what he was for Aristotle: a living animal with the capacity for a political existence; modern man is an animal whose politics places his existence as a living being in question."

It is against the relief of the emerging and developing biopolitics of the eighteenth and nineteenth centuries that Nietzsche's comments on the *life-giving* and *life-taking* powers of music begin to make more sense. While some might be inclined merely to dismiss Nietzsche's comments regarding Wagner's music as the aesthetic rantings of a philosopher who's well-known falling out with his former friend have tainted his appreciation of the composer, the emerging biopolitics indicated by Foucault provide an important and different context in which to understand them.

If Foucault is accurate in his assessment that the issue of measuring and calculating what fosters life and disallows it to the point of death is a major social and political preoccupation of the period, then Nietzsche's observations on the music of Wagner are prime fodder to begin a discussion of a biopolitics of music.

For example, Nietzsche's comments that the music of Wagner is harmful to one's health and makes people sick might be understood through the context of the emerging social and political concerns and controls over the health of society. What might have seemed without biopolitics as a passing *aesthetic* jab at Wagner by Nietzsche becomes through the context of a biopolitics a commentary on the health of society. It also suggests that the philosopher's comment that *Nietzsche contra Wagner* is not a book for Germans and that he does not have reader's in Germany entails that because the music of Wagner is championed in this country, its people, like the composer and his music, are sick and unhealthy.

Nietzsche explains in some detail in *Nietzsche contra Wagner* the difference between "healthy" and "unhealthy" music. It is a difference that is not grounded in aesthetics, but is rather based in physiology:

> My objections to the music of Wagner are physiological objections: why should I trouble to dress them up in aesthetic formulas? After all, aesthetics is nothing but a kind of applied physiology.

This notion of aesthetics as a "kind of applied physiology," turns up later in the twentieth-century in efforts to measure the effects of music on people and to use these effects as a form of control over them. The classic example here is "Musak," which was created in 1922 to provide music over the telephone, but then branched out in 1940 into selling atmosphere music.

For Nietzsche, however, the physiological "fact" of Wagner's music is quite clear:

> My "fact," my *petit fait vrai*, is that I no longer breathe easily when this music begins to affect me; that my foot soon resents

137

it and rebels: my foot feels the need for rhythm, dance, march—to Wagner's "Kaiser-marsch" not even the young German Kaiser could march—it demands of music first of all those delights which are found in good walking, striding, dancing. But does not my stomach protest too? my heart? my circulation? Are not my entrails saddened? Do I not suddenly become hoarse? To listen to Wagner I need pastilles Gérandel.

It is important to note that Nietzsche's comments here are not about his "emotional" response to the music of Wagner, but rather about its "affect."

Brian Massumi describes the difference in his book, *Politics of Affect* (2015)—a difference that might be used to explicate Nietzsche's comment:

> you have to understand affect as something other than simply a personal feeling. By "affect" I don't mean emotion in the everyday sense. The way I use it comes primarily from Spinoza. He talks of the body in terms of its capacity for affecting and being affected. These are not two different capacities—they always go together. When you affect something, you are at the same time opening yourself up to being affected in turn, and in a slightly different way than you might have been the moment before. You have made a transition, however slight. You have stepped over a threshold. Affect is this passing of a threshold, seen from the point of view of the change in capacity. It's crucial to remember that Spinoza uses this to talk about the body. What a body is, he says, is what it can do as it goes along.

Thus, the problem with the music of Wagner according to Nietzsche is its *affect* on his body: it makes him breathe uneasily, upsets his stomach, pains his heart, changes the circulation of his blood, makes him so hoarse that he requires a throat lozenge (pastilles Gérandel) to ease his physical discomfort.

The trouble here is that these are not the bodily affects Nietzsche "expects of music":

And so I ask myself: What is it that my whole body really expects of music? For there is no soul. I believe, its own *ease*: as if all animal functions should be quickened by easy, bold, exuberant, self-assured rhythms; as if iron, leaden life should lose its gravity through golden, tender, oil-smooth melodies. My melancholy wants to rest in hiding-places and abysses of *perfection*: that is why I need music. But Wagner makes sick.

The implications of Nietzsche's comments on the music of Wagner regarding a politics of life are manifest: music has power over life. Some music *eases* our body, whereas other music does the opposite, that is, *dis*-eases our body. This power of music over life extends to populations as well. It is, in the words of Foucault, "massifying." The fact that the people of Germany adore the music of Wagner is for Nietzsche a statement in itself on their overall health.

Though the "physiological objections" to the music of Wagner appear in the philosopher's final book, *Nietzsche contra Wagner*, they were first published in his 1882 book, *The Gay Science*, and then again in its revised edition in 1887. Though very similar to the wording in *Nietzsche contra Wagner*, the philosopher noticeably omits the final paragraph of the section, which is stylistically set as a parenthetical reply from the Wagnerian:

> (I forgot to mention how my enlightened Wagnerian replied to these physiological objections: "Then you really are merely not healthy enough for our music?")

This final thought in *The Gay Science* brings us back to the matter of affect and capacity. Like Spinoza, Nietzsche views the body in terms of its capacity for affecting *and* being affected. However, Nietzsche's comments on Wagner open up the added dimension of considering the body in terms of its capacity for affecting *music* as well as its being affected by it. Thus, the question "Then you really are merely not healthy enough for our music?" arguably concerns both the domains of affect and biopolitics.

Now that Nietzsche has helped us to open up a space to consider the biopolitics of music, I'll leave it to the reader to ask which musicians today "make music sick." Or, if you prefer, to pursue a related one—What *writers* today "make writing sick?"

139

17 | HAS LITERATURE
RUN OUT OF STEAM?

Making literature in the twenty-first century is a very different than making literature in the twentieth century. Some of the differences can be traced back to changes in the book industry that began in the previous century when the neoliberal economic policies of Ronald Reagan in the United States and Margaret Thatcher in Britain in the 1980s spurred an increase in mergers and acquisitions of book publishers. Whereas in the 1960s, there were 183 mergers or acquisitions of book publishers, and, in the 1970s, there were 177, the uptick in the 1980s to 213 was only a portent of the 516 mergers or acquisitions in the 1990s that fundamentally changed the business of books—and by extension, the making of contemporary literature.

The second-wave neoliberal-nineties of Bill Clinton's market globalism in the U.S. and Tony Blair's Third Way in the UK carried over into the new millennium, and infamously burst when the stock market crashed in 2008. By this time, the corporate book industry was one where twelve publishers out of approximately 85,000 accounted for almost two-thirds of U.S. trade and mass market book sales; where 90 percent of active publishers accounted for less than 10 percent of total book sales; and where Random House alone accounted for over 13 percent of all U.S. book sales, a figure that put just this one company's total book sales as *exceeding* the book sales of more than 76,000 U.S. trade and mass market publishers *combined*.

But if economic changes in the book industry were the only ones that differentiated the making of twenty-first century from twentieth-century literature, the story of making literature now would be a fairly easy one to calculate or tell. Unfortunately, however, they are not. The story of making literature in the twenty-first century has been further complicated by the dawn of the ebook age and the advent of digital publishing software. The former should be dated back to 2007, when Amazon released its first Kindle Readers. It was also the same year that the amazing Espresso Book Machine was introduced at BookExpo America, a machine that allowed individuals to "print out" fully bound books—a technology that was only possible through advances in digital publishing software.

Amidst all this new technology of book production, reproduction, and distribution arose a new revolution in publishing: the self-publishing revolution. Whereas in 2007 there were about 75,000 self-published titles, by 2015 (and the latest data currently[7] available), this number has risen to 727,125 self-published titles produced in just one year. In short, a combination of technological and economic changes has fundamentally altered—if not "revolutionized"—the way books are produced, reproduced, and distributed. To be sure, the twenty-first century is an exciting time to take up the question of how literature is made *now*, especially since more literature is published annually today than at any other point in book history.

Amy Hungerford's *Making Literature Now* offers an "intriguing" approach to the contemporary outpouring of literature today.[8] "Intriguing" because Hungerford sees the "social" world and "making" of contemporary literature in a theoretically unique and daunting way albeit one that affords the technological advances and economic factors a more significant role in the making of literature than more traditional accounts of contemporary literature.

Drawing upon the sociology of Bruno Latour, Hungerford believes that

> social connections only deserve the name when they are acted upon, that the social only exists at all when its networks are activated, and what's more, the social actors come in both human and nonhuman forms. Our connections to other people only constitute social organization when we, or nonhuman actors like books, apps, or delivery truck routes, act to change or shape the arrangements in which we live—be they material, cultural, environmental, geographic, psychic, intellectual.

She acknowledges though that this method of inquiry can be "daunting and tedious and threaten to devolve into what one colleague called 'a heap of facts': being *there* to see the conversations that make things happen in whatever field of endeavor we want to understand; raking the archives not for recollection or record but for the actual trace of a social act as it unfolded, and not just one social act but an infinite series of them; cramming them, by force of method, into the book one writes." Consequently, application of Latour's method, termed "Actor-Network-Theory" (or simply, "ANT"), yields for Hungerford a much finer-grained response to questions regarding the making of literature. Simple statements about its production say from its author or editor are rejected as methodologically unsound when considered outside of the wider network of actors involved in its making. Moreover, even the use of extensive interviews and archival research on the literature in question to produce an account of its making can fall short of the methodological bar set by ANT.

Out of the 85,000 publishers extant today, Hungerford selects one of the relatively smaller ones to focus on in her account of how literature is made now. The first two chapters of her book are devoted to McSweeney's literary quarterly and press, a non-profit publishing house founded in 1998 by Dave Eggers that is distributed all over the world. Given that "533 different writers appeared in the first 31 issues . . . and thousands of others read their work," McSweeney's is, for her, an especially rich little magazine and press from which to gain a sense of "contemporary" American publishing (even though Hungerford prefers "post-1945" or "20th century" to describe the field of the "contemporary").

Viewing McSweeney's from the point of view of social networks and regarding non-human actors such as the technologies of publication (e.g. Aldus Pagemaker, Adobe PageMaker) and apps (e.g. the subscription app created for McSweeney's by Russell Quinn) yields a much different account of the little magazine than simple pronouncements about it from its editor—even a celebrity one such as Eggers. ANT allows Hungerford to treat "the subscription" and "the iPhone" as "actors" in the story of the rise of McSweeney's on the same par as its editors, authors, and readers. It also allows her to widen the social network around this little magazine to include not only its celebrity authors such as David Foster Wallace, Rick Moody and Eggers himself, but also its "subsistence writers" and "volunteer,

143

part-time literati."

But Hungerford is also emphatic that this method *should not* be applied to just any little magazine or writer. Rather, it should be applied to celebrity little magazines and writers, rather than failed ones. Why? Because stories about failed or briefly-known little magazines and writers

> lack the intrinsic attraction of accounts that focus on the charismatic, the successful, and the well known. Insofar as the failed or only briefly visible writers vastly outnumber the successful ones, and insofar as it doesn't take much in the way of disaster to stop most of us from writing our novel, their stories may lack both interest and individuality; the banality of failure doesn't make for good reading.

For the majority of participants in the world of literature, that is those who are editors of "uncelebrated" little magazines and authors of "briefly visible" or "failed" books, Hungerford's claim will probably raise some ire—or at least the hair on the back of their necks. Why should this work be excluded from accounts of the making of literature now? After all, celebrity and fame are not the stuff of most books and publishers in America. And also, isn't failure often as good a teacher as success?

Hungerford's claim here is somewhat peculiar too considering that while McSweeney's has its charms, it is hardly the powerful press of the most celebrated and well-known authors in contemporary American literature, which comes to the fore when one puts the author list of say Random House next to McSweeney's.

But these provisos aside, if we view her comment as part of a wider culture that is obsessed with "stars" and "celebrity," rather than the opposite, then it makes more sense. After all, celebrity culture now seems to overrun just about every facet of American life—so why not the study of literature too? And, given the tedium of an ANT account, it is probably best to counter-balance this by applying it to the well-known and charismatic—in the hope of making this type of literary scholarship more exciting its readers.

Hungerford makes a strong case in *Making Literature Now* both against traditional "close-reading," and in favor of what might be called "surface reading." The argument against close-reading, made at different points throughout the book, amounts to the fact that close-reading does not provide us with much insight into the network in which little magazines or literature function, that is, drawing on Franco Moretti, Hungerford says "traditional closed reading is blind to the fabric." For that matter, even if we advocated for close reading, to perform it on just the "actual literary production of a single year of the 19th century would take many lifetimes" states Hungerford, let alone the 55,000 novels that were published in just 2010. And set against 727,125 self-published books in 2015, the rationale seems even more reasonable.

Her point about limited close-reading time comes up again most notoriously in the final chapter of the book, "On Not Reading DFW." After submitting a negative piece on David Foster Wallace to the *LA Review of Books*, one that provided some balance to the "Saint Dave phenomenon," the editor told Hungerford, in response to her argument as to why she does not want to read more Wallace, that she needed to read *more* Wallace. Focusing on his personal misogyny, and "[t]he fact that Wallace makes a subject out this aspect of his behavior," she refuses to read any more of his writing—even though he is "intermittently regretful about his behavior toward women." She decided that further reading of Wallace would be a poor use of her time—and wrote an article defending her decision. The editor's comment that she needed to read more Wallace (to convince her that she needed to continue to read Wallace) assumed "that a refusal can't, in the absence of more reading, have an intellectual or scholarly relationship to a professional decision about resource allocation—about what to spend one's (limited) time doing."

Understand, Hungerford is not telling *us* that we should not read Wallace, but rather stating and defending her own position, which of course she is more than entitled to do. What is even more interesting about her refusal (and an editor's response to it) is that she refuses to read Wallace while at the same time is serving on a doctoral committee at Yale University, where she is a professor of English and Dean of Humanities, for a graduate student who is writing on recovery culture—and using Wallace's *Infinite Jest*. "For me, the most persuasive of reasons to be interested in Wallace right now is that as Jamison's [doctoral] advisor I want to be in conversation with her, and to be the best conversation partner I can be might in the end require that I read Wallace's novel," states Hungerford. "My respect

145

for Jamison as a writer and thinker makes me open to the task."

One would think too that her respect for the integrity of the doctoral program at her university might also make her "open" to reading a work on which her student is researching and writing. But this does not seem to be a consideration—at least not in this chapter. The primary thing that seems to matter here is the extension of her personal disrespect and refusal to read more Wallace even when faced with the professional responsibility of directing a doctoral dissertation. Whether or not one agrees with Hungerford's decision not to read any more Wallace, the situation she describes with her doctoral student takes her refusal from the personal (using our limited reading-time well) to the professional (what are our obligations to our graduate students). And from each perspective, the decision appears different. Moreover, while Hungerford prefers to foreground the personal reasons, others might be more interested in the professional ones, especially as they relate in general to the conditions of our professional obligation to read authors and works that we find personally repugnant.

A similar dilemma is described in the preceding chapter regarding Jonathan Safran Foer's novel *Everything Is Illuminated*, which she describes as "an aesthetic innovation within the history of American Holocaust narratives." For Hungerford, Foer's generation of Holocaust writing is "a field not defined by the original genres and their cultural stature—or by the tighter relational bond of parent and child, with its accompanying filial pieties." It "is defined rather by questions of personal achievement and recognition in a network of values that distill out of the larger batch of new writers a subgroup we might call the bi-coastal young literati."

The literature of this field is not one that often sits well with scholars of contemporary literature for it is one in which "writing remains a prestigious avenue to fame" and celebrity. Or, in the case of Foer, is motivated by a need for "attention" (and for Hungerford, "*Foer loves attention*"). Still, despite its vain motivations—or perhaps *because* of them, it was selected by her students to be the final novel in her "American Novel since 1945" course. "I had to read it," writes Hungerford, "and deliver two fresh lectures." "My students' love—produced by and mediated through the literary press, peer sociality, and the classroom—produced, if not exactly more love, then at least more attention"—for, of course, Foer. One is tempted though to ask why "I had to read it" holds for the classroom scenario but not for the dissertation situation, especially since the Foer chapter comes before the Wallace chapter in her book.

The middle two chapters of *Making Literature Now* focus on the use of the net and apps to produce innovative and interesting ways of reading (or relating with) and making literature. However, the Small Demons web venture she describes in Chapter 3 is now "closed" and the Red Lemonade web site "appears, as of this writing, to be inactive." Still, her account in Chapter 4 of the serialized, exploratory novel for iPad and iPhone, *The Silent History* (in spite of its unfortunate publication as a bound book by Farrar, Straus and Giroux in 2014)—is one of the highlights of the volume as it persuasively demonstrates how human and nonhuman "actors" can participate in a network that is making literature now.

Making Literature Now demonstrates well the impact of little magazines in the making of literature—and celebrity. Moreover, the effective and convincing use of actor-network-theory by Hungerford in the cause of understanding contemporary (or "post-1945") literature is very persuasive, and begs for more applications of this approach. And not just to "celebrated" networks such as McSweeney's, but to others such as the *LA Review of Books* (which rejected her DFW essay) and the *American Book Review* (which would have published it, if it had been offered to them). For that matter, if celebrity and fame *should* be considerations (as Hungerford argues) for applying ANT to literature, then those publishers and magazines which truly *are* the homes to the "famous" and well-known" writers like *The New Yorker* and Random House publishing corporation are perhaps even more appropriate places to apply this demanding yet effective method.

Hungerford raises the bar on accounts of how literature is made and how we tell the story of little magazines now. Her book shows how making literature now involves far more than simply an artist or author as sole actor or creative genius. Rather, literature now involves a range of actors—both human and nonhuman—put into a dynamic network of creative possibility. This is especially important given changes in the way books are produced, reproduced, and distributed. ANT allows non-human factors to be treated on an equal par with human ones, which is important when considering literature

147

as part of a larger fabric or complex network of actors. The ways of describing making literature now in Hungerford's book teases us with the possibilities of using a similar approach on other works and authors, celebrated or otherwise.

While the range of presses, magazines, and authors covered by Hungerford tells only a small part of the huge story as to how literature comes to be today, it is nevertheless a significant one because it can serve as a model for future ANT-style interventions into literature. Also, the highly personal reasons for reading and not reading provided by Hungerford in light of the fact that more literature is being produced today than ever before in book history are a sobering statement on the difficulties of being a scholar of contemporary literature. While it makes me nervous to say that we should *only* do "surface reading" when examining contemporary literature, the rationale for this proposal in light of book overproduction today is a well meaning and pragmatic one.

Hungerford's *Making Literature Now* is engaging reading and will kindle much debate for years to come. It raises a host of important issues for scholars of contemporary literature—not the least of which is how they should approach the intimidating and growing mountain of magazines, books, and authors in circulation today. Hungerford's opening argument that those that do not rise to the level of celebrity or are failures are not worth our consideration though still needs to be reconciled with her closing argument that reading one of the most celebrated and successful writers of the last twenty-five years is not worth her time—especially since writers that she resists, such as Wallace and Foer, are of major interest to students and scholars of literature now.

18 | THE BLOOMING
OF AMERICAN LITERATURE

Emerson is the *Ursuppe* of American literature, or, so argues Harold
Bloom in *The American Canon*, a collection of essays he wrote over a
span of fifty years.[9] Everything that is *great* about American literature
stems back to Emerson—and everything that is not so great about
it ignores or rejects Emerson. Thus, the "problems" of American
literature for Bloom are always already Emersonian: "The problem of
American poetry after Emerson might be defined as 'Is it possible to
be un-Emersonian, rather than, at best, anti-Emersonian?'" However,
in spite of the grand claims for Emerson's influence over American
literature in *The American Canon*, collected and edited by David Mikics,
he is nowhere to be found in Bloom's final book published during his
lifetime, *Possessed by Memory*—and it is no small book.[10]

Five hundred and eight pages spaced over seventy-five chapters
with discussions spanning the Hebrew Bible to twentieth-century
American poetry with significant detours through Shakespeare and
the British romantics, but no chapter in *Possessed by Memory* devoted
to Emerson. Not even a few pages. In Part Four, "The Imperfect Is
Our Paradise: Walt Whitman and Twentieth-Century American
Poetry," there are three chapters on Wallace Stevens, two chapters
on Whitman, and individual chapters on Edwin Arlington Robinson,
William Carlos Williams, Archie Randolph Ammons, Hart Crane,
Conrad Aiken, Richard Eberhart, Weldon Kees, May Swenson,
Delmore Schwartz, Alvin Feinman, John Ashbery, John Wheelwright,
James Merrill, Jay Macpherson, and Amy Clampitt. Given the way
Emerson becomes the measure of all literature in America in *The
American Canon*, his significant lack of presence in *Possessed by Memory*
is more than a little bit surprising.

In *Possessed by Memory*, Bloom tells us that the lifelong model
for his criticism is Samuel Johnson, who taught him "that criticism, as
a literary art, belongs to the ancient genre of wisdom writing." "The
deepest lesson," he learned from Johnson, "is that any authority of
criticism as a literary genre must depend on the human wisdom of

the critic, not upon the wrongness or rightness of either theory or praxis." And, recall again, that in *Possessed by Memory*, Bloom also called upon Oscar Wilde's "The Critic as Artist" (1891), where he wrote, "the highest criticism really is, the record of one's own soul." For Bloom, just as for Wilde, this type of criticism is both "more fascinating than history, as it is concerned simply with oneself," and "more delightful than philosophy, as its subject is concrete and not abstract, real not vague." But, alas, by Wilde's own contention, the "highest criticism" is also merely "autobiography, as it deals not with events, but with the thoughts of one's life; not with life's physical accidents of deed or circumstance, but with the spiritual moods and imaginative passions of the mind." Mix Johnson and Wilde along with some William Hazlitt, John Ruskin, Walter Pater, William James, Kenneth Burke—and Ralph Waldo Emerson—and you have Bloom's self-professed form of criticism—criticism that ultimately is accountable only to him. So, while Emerson is acknowledged as vital to his critical approach to literature in *Possessed by Memory*, he is presented on a par with James and Burke in terms of significant critical influences from the American tradition.

Given that the essays in *The American Canon* were written by Bloom, there is no denying that as a collection they present a consistent argument regarding the role of Emerson in American literature. Every author discussed in the volume is in one way or another measured against Emerson. These writings were selected primarily from among seven of Bloom's over fifty books of literary criticism: *The Ringers in the Tower: Studies in the Romantic Tradition* (1971), *Wallace Stevens: The Poems of Our Climate* (1976), *Figures of Capable Imagination* (1976), *Poetics of Influence: New and Selected Criticism* (1988), *How to Read and Why* (2000), *Genius: A Mosaic of One Hundred Exemplary Creative Minds* (2002), and *The Daemon Knows: Literary Greatness and the American Sublime* (2015). Still, given the lack of emphasis on Emerson in *Possessed by Memory*, particularly in Part Four, where American poetry is extensively discussed and where Whitman and Stevens dominate his American literature attention not Emerson, the argument of *The American Canon* feels constructed *post hoc*, that is, contrived—not sincere. And while there is plenty of mention of Kenneth Burke in *The American Canon*, especially to passing conversations and opinions on various

American authors shared by Burke with Bloom, William James is virtually absent from the volume (even though his brother, Henry James, plays a heavy role in assessing the American novel).

I point this out because no one would doubt, say, the devotion of Richard Poirier or Stanley Cavell to Emerson's philosophy. Their thought runs in and through these two thinkers consistently and unequivocally. In the same way, there is little doubt as to the role of say, Samuel Johnson, the Hebrew Bible, Shakespeare, the English Romantic poets, and Sigmund Freud in the life and thought of Bloom. Emerson too plays a role, but in the American canon he is secondary to many other authors for Bloom including Whitman, Hart Crane, and Wallace Stevens. Again, the proof of this is established by *Possessed by Memory*, not *The American Canon*, which portrays Emerson as Bloom's American literature *abgrund*. The former book is a map of the inner life of Harold Bloom, one of the most well-read, original, and prolific critics of *any* generation; by comparison, the latter is a memento from the external life of Harold Bloom, the literary industry who edited hundreds of anthologies for Chelsea House and who produced scores of popular literary books for profit (sometimes quite significant) beginning over a ten year period in the late-twentieth and early-twenty-first centuries with titles such as *The Western Canon: The Books and School of the Ages* (1994), *How to Read and Why* (2000), *Stories and Poems for Extremely Intelligent Children of All Ages* (2001), and *Genius: A Mosaic of One Hundred Exemplary Creative Minds* (2003)—until his death in 2019. In these works, many written for a general audience, Bloom's critical gift is far too often reduced to empty and mean-spirited pronouncements of "greatness" or "canonicity."

For example, in pages drawn from these mass market performances regarding American drama, Bloom uses the "greatness" trope to take down an entire branch of American literature in one sentence: "It is a sad and inexplicable truth that the United States, a dramatic nation, continues to have so limited a literary achievement in drama."

Moreover, of two of American drama's principle figures, Eugene O'Neill and Henry Miller, snipes Bloom, both write "very badly," with the former described as "leaden" and the latter as "drab." Though we are presumably shielded in *The American Canon* from writers for which Bloom had "mixed feelings" (Mikics says in his editorial Preface that he focuses on American writers "about whom Bloom has made his strongest, most memorable arguments, and have omitted some well-known figures toward whom he has displayed mixed feelings in his criticism"), his treatment of drama reveals both the limits of his nativist-aesthetic critical approach to American literature ("O'Neill's ancestry . . . has little to do with American tradition, with Emerson or William James or any other of our cultural spectators. Schopenhauer, Nietzsche, and Freud formed O'Neill's sense of what little was possible for any of us") and the nadir of his critical acumen in this book ("insofar as O'Neill's art is nonverbal it must also be nonexistent").

It troubles me to see American drama so cavalierly dismissed *in toto* by Bloom, which includes not just O'Neil and Miller, but also the dramatic contributions of Edward Albee, Luis Alfaro, Amiri Baraka, Lorraine Hansberry, Lillian Hellman, Langston Hughes, David Henry Hwang, Tony Kushner, Clare Boothe Luce, David Mamet, Terrence McNally, José Rivera, Sam Shepard, Neil Simon, Luis Valdez, Thornton Wilder, Tennessee Williams, August Wilson, Lanford Wilson, Karen Zacarias, Mary Zimmerman, and many others. I mention these American playwrights not because they are extensively discussed in the book (they are not—only Albee, O'Neill, and Williams get chapters). But rather, they are noted here so that the scope and scale of what is summarily dismissed by Bloom can begin to be identified. Bloom's America and its literary canon as presented in this volume includes no authors born after the 1930s. It is also tone deaf to the aesthetic innovation and cultural diversity that shaped much twentieth-century American literature into world literature in the new millennium. The traditional American road back to Emerson may, for example, be present in say August Wilson or Mary Zimmerman. However, as a measure of their drama today, it is a road that is critically superfluous to the standards of literary criticism in the second decade of the new millennium.

As the direct influence of Emerson comes to be more remote in the writers who were born in the twentieth century and who are discussed by Bloom, other considerations need to be brought to bear such as intersectional issues of race, class, gender, and sexuality. Here the work of literary theory and cultural studies has had remarkable success, particularly since the mid-1970s, in bringing a whole new perspective on American literature and its canon. Bloom, of course, will have nothing of it in these essays. Passing growls at political correctness are commonplace in the volume (e.g., of Marianne Moore, "Some day she will remind us also of what current cultural politics obscure: that any distinction between poetry written by women or poetry by men is a mere polemic, unless it follows upon an initial distinction between good and bad poetry"). Plentiful too are *ad hoc* attacks on literary theory (e.g., of Toni Morrison, who is described as "a self-proclaimed African American Marxist and feminist" in whose work he "hear[s] a totalizing ideology," but believes that "to read in the service of any ideology is not to read at all").

Oddly enough though, in spite of Bloom's repeated insistence that ideology has no role in literary criticism, he added references to the politics of U. S. President Donald J. Trump to a number of the chapters. The most extensive is a long quotation from a wild speech President Trump gave on October 18, 2018 ("Democrats produce mobs. Republicans produce jobs. It's true. It's true. By the way, this is the most beautiful sky. Well, it's a big sky. I guess there is a reason for everything, right?"), which Bloom says Nathaniel West "as a ghost, inspired or wrote these presidential remarks." He concludes his chapter on West saying, "Perhaps West's ghost now writes not only Shagpokian speeches, but the very text of reality in our America." While Bloom is convincing regarding the power of West's "satirical genius" and that his ghost haunts Trump, his move to ideological critique at key points in the volume has the effect of reducing in power (if not entirely obviating) his aestheticism.

Moreover, Bloom's continuous attacks, for example, on gender studies and ideological criticism, serve only to draw his work closer in affiliation to the New Criticism, his self-professed critical nemesis in this volume than further away from it. His critical disagreements with T. S. Eliot, whose work is widely championed by the New Criticism, center in part on Eliot's "scorn for Emerson," which Bloom views "is so ill-informed that some personal bias has to be noted in it." Though Eliot's poetry "ravished" Bloom's ear when he was a "child," his prose "still displeases [him]." The complexities of Bloom's love-hate relationship to Eliot serves as a thin line that distances his work from the New Criticism. Nevertheless, with the passage of time, the joint devotion to aestheticism of Bloom and the New Critics has drawn their work closer together in the historical imagination of the critical tradition.

153

Throughout the volume much effort is placed by Bloom on distinguishing his work from the likes of Allen Tate, Cleanth Brooks, and Robert Penn Warren rather than Roland Barthes, Jacques Derrida, and Michel Foucault. In short, the legacies of the New Criticism and his relationship to it occupy all of his critical attention, rather than the futures of poststructuralism, which we can now say in retrospect have had a far greater influence on most contemporary developments in literary and cultural theory than the New Criticism (the major exceptions here being postcritique, object-oriented ontology, and radical aestheticism). This pattern continues as well in his use and view of Emerson—one that today feels dated compared to the work of some his contemporaries. This is not just because he insists on using Emerson as the measure of *all* American literature, but rather *how* Bloom uses Emerson.

In the hands of Richard Poirier, for example in his 1992 book, *Poetry and Pragmatism,* "Emersonian pragmatism has more affinities with post-structuralist than with modernist theory." This allows Poirier to make points about the canonical status of texts that avoid talk of "permanent" authors. "Indeed, works tend to remain canonical," comments Poirier, "not because of their alleged dalliance with political or social stabilities, but because of their own linguistic instability, their tendency to slip their moorings and thus to encourage alternative interpretations, continually over time." Argues Poirier, "a strong, particularly energizing mode of linguistic skepticism was already available to those who had learned to appreciate the distrusts of language implicit in the anti-foundationalism of Charles Peirce or William James or John Dewey, or who, even without exposure to these philosophers or to Santayana or Cavell, had otherwise come to appreciate the movements of language in Stein, Stevens, or Frost."

Now compare Poirier's approach to the canon in the American tradition to Bloom's:

> [Robert] Hayden is a permanent poet, canonical in a sense that current politicism continues to deride. Cultural fashions fade away, and literary survival always depends upon three criteria: aesthetic splendor, cognitive power, and wisdom. A time will come when much current rant and cant will dwindle into period pieces, at best.

Both Bloom and Poirier share an affinity for some of the same thinkers—Emerson, James, and Burke—however they use them to differing ends. Bloom bludgeons contemporary theory with them by reading Emerson as an "experiential critic and essayist, and not a Transcendental philosopher" who shaped the American literary canon; Poirier, however, recognizing that most of them "have been afforded little or no place in the history of contemporary theory," provides them with a place through linguistic skepticism. Question is which Emerson and American tradition should prevail: one founded upon "aesthetic splendor, cognitive power, and wisdom" or one founded on a distrust of language?

My preference as a contemporary theorist who values American philosophy from Emerson to Rorty is to bring this philosophy into dialogue with both the literature of America *and* contemporary theory. More importantly, to show that the writings of these American thinkers contribute more than just a means to an individually rich life, but rather can help us to address and work through the problems facing our own society and the world. Bloom's highest criticism yields an American canon unable to appreciate in full the tapestry of aesthetic *and* social and political contributions of our literature. His resistance to theory is a resistance to the world in which we now live and for which we must take on increasing degrees of responsibility. To take shelter in an Emerson who as an "experiential critic" appears to have no other concern with society and the world aside from how it impacts his own "self-reliance" is to neglect the worldly philosophical one who wondered in his journal amidst the panic of 1837, just a few months before he delivered "The American Scholar," his justly celebrated Phi Beta Kappa address, "Is the world sick?" Two days later, he continues: "The black times have a great scientific value. It is an epoch so critical a philosopher would not miss." This is Emerson the critical *philosopher* speaking—the one that has been far too often neglected in the type of criticism Bloom advocates.

I agree with Bloom that a higher criticism that is solely "the record of one's own soul" can be generated on the basis of Emerson's thoughts. But so too can philosophies like the linguistic skepticism of Poirier that embrace contemporary theory or like that of Stanley Cavell, who in his 1989 book, *This New Yet Unapproachable America*, finds in Emerson that "philosophy has to do with the perplexed capacity to mourn the passing of the world." Thus, for Cavell, rather than turning his back on ethics, politics, and the world, Emerson as *philosopher* makes major contributions to these areas of concern. All of which is to say, Bloom's higher criticism presents us with a choice regarding Emerson and the American canon: to view it from the perspective of his higher criticism which rejects theory and philosophy; or to accept him as a philosopher and theorist, and to welcome his uniquely American vision of philosophy.

"The question concerning Emerson's standing in or for philosophy," comments Cavell, "is meant to question what is I believe the most widely fixated, critical gesture toward Emerson both on the part of his friends and of his enemies, from the time of James Russell Lowell in *A Fable for Critics* in 1848 to Harold Bloom in *The New York Review of Books* in 1984, in a review entitled 'Mr. America,' namely *the gesture of denying to Emerson the title of philosopher*" (my emphasis). In addition, Cavell points out that the denial of Emerson as philosopher also comes with the view of his "prose as a kind of mist or fog," a view of Emerson that he attributes to Bloom.

For Cavell, Emerson believes that "philosophy is to be overcome," but not rejected. So, what then does Emerson favor in place of philosophy? Writes Cavell, Emerson is

> Not in favor, evidently, of science or poetry or religion, from each of which this writing distinguishes itself. In favor, then, of philosophy itself, in the face of the completed edifice of philosophy as system and as necessary, unified foundation. Every European philosopher since Hegel has felt he must inherit this edifice and/or destroy it; no American philosopher has such a relation to the history of philosophy.

To be sure, Emerson as philosopher, either in the sense of Poirier or Cavell, is not a position that Bloom supports. Why? Because Emerson as philosopher simply does not fit the protocols of his higher criticism, which is, decidedly, not a form of philosophy.

"Criticism," states Bloom, "is as much a series of metaphors for the acts of loving what we have read as for the acts of reading themselves." "I am an experiential and personalizing literary critic," he writes, "which certainly rouses up enmity, but I go on believing that poems matter only if we matter." But by fashioning one of America's most original and powerful philosophers in the image of himself, namely, as an "experiential critic," Bloom does a disservice to the rich and original history that is American philosophy from Emerson to Rorty.

The limits of Bloom's highly personal form of criticism are much less obvious when he is wandering through the Bible, Shakespeare, Milton, and British romantic poetry in pursuance of his inward critical journey as opposed to when this criticism is turned specifically to American literature. In the case of *Possessed by Memory*, there is no effort by Bloom to convince the reader that he is doing anything more than tracing the sublime visionary affects of literature on him. *Possessed by Memory* is a record of the spiritual moods and imaginative passions of Bloom's fertile mind—a record that can be fascinating reading for those who desire for one reason or the other to be his critical passengers. But for those seeking to learn more about American literature, particularly in the age of Trump, *The American Canon* does not offer very much insight.

Bloom's writing on American literature is a time capsule of a very different and dated approach to literature. To get a sense of this difference, try using one of Bloom's lines at a major academic conference: "[Philip] Roth has earned a permanent place in American literature by a comic genius that need never be doubted again." Based on the angry reaction of the entire large audience to a similar statement at a recent #MeToo panel, there is nothing permanent or funny about Roth's misogyny. *The American Canon* reveals well the long petrification process of a prolific and influential critic who refused to adapt his criticism to contemporary standards and who reveled in the enmity his "archaic Romantic" higher criticism often elicited. *The American Canon* convinces me that the philosophical Emerson, whether of Poirier or Cavell, is always preferable to the "experiential critic" one of Bloom.

157

19 | PHILOSOPHY WITHOUT APOLOGIES

"I do not know what effect my accusers have had upon you, gentlemen, but for my own part I was almost carried away by them; their arguments were so convincing. On the other hand, scarcely a word of what they said was true."

—Opening lines of Plato's *The Apology of Socrates*

Western philosophy began with an apology. Will it end though when we lose our desire and ability to apologize? If so, then philosophy is in big trouble today.

Few public figures seem interested now in thoughtfully, carefully, and deliberately defending themselves against alleged wrongdoing.

Moreover, among the publicly accused, there seems to be a general lack of understanding as to why their accusers would even think they have done something wrong.

It is common now for alleged wrongdoers to mindlessly reply to their accusers, "I'm sorry you're offended by my actions."

But this is not an "apology." It is though a new genre: the "non-apology apology."

It may be linked to the Western philosophical tradition with what is called "egoism," the view that we should consider only ourselves and that any consideration of others is solely based on self-interest.

So, when the "egoist" offers their "non-apology apology," saying "I'm sorry you're offended by my actions," they are really not admitting to doing *anything* wrong.

Moreover, in saying that they are "sorry" if their actions have caused any offense, what they mean is that they are not sorry for you. Rather, they are sorry for themselves *because they have to make this "(non-apology) apology" to you.*

In the Western philosophical tradition, there has of course been much discussion of egoism, but it is a position that really has been

159

relegated to the dustbin of bad ideas, that is, until now.

One of the legacies of the early twenty-first century will be the spread of the belief that egoism coupled with optimism and aggression is a desirable personal identity and form of conduct. Today, we call the person who with aggression and optimism considers only themselves, and who believes that any consideration of others must be based on self-interest, the "neoliberal man." As such, we might also call the "non-apology apology" the neoliberal man offers as simply the "neoliberal apology."

In contemporary popular culture, one of the best examples of the neoliberal man and his fate is Walter White of the television series *Breaking Bad.* Though White spends much of the series trying to convince himself and others that his heinous and violent actions were altruistic, that is, done out of a concern for his family's future, he admits by the end of the series that this was not true—and that everything he (that is, Heisenberg) did was about fulfilling his own self-interest.

The purely neoliberal man makes *no apologies* for his actions.

Money, fame, ego, aggression, self-interest, and complete disregard for the welfare of others are the modus operandi of the neoliberal man.

Some regard him as a menace to society who needs to be called to justice.

Others see the neoliberal man as a hero who should not be accountable to the law.

I, however, see him as an individual who acts without apology outside of the mandates of Western philosophy, which is, after all, a form of philosophy that was steeped in the apology.

ॐ

In Greek, "apologia" means "a defense" or "a speech in defense." The most well-known from the ancient Greek period is the "apology" Socrates gave when he was publicly accused of wrong doing in 399 BCE.

But "apologies" in a philosophical sense need not be limited to the courtroom or formal "defenses" of one's opinions. It is also fair to say that every argument that uses logic and reason to defend a position is an apologia. The case of Socrates though sets the high bar for apologias.

Socrates was considered by some a menace to society. Three citizens of Athens brought a public action against him. Their names were Meletus, Anytus, and Lycon.

The specific charges for which he stood trial were heresy—or "impiety," if you will—and corrupting the youth of Athens.

His "defense" against these charges was faithfully and respectfully recounted by his student Plato after his death in a work simply entitled "Apology," one of the seminal texts of early Western philosophy.

Athenians like Socrates regarded debates as a form of recreation, and flocked to the Assembly and the courts to hear them. These debates were part of the life-blood of Athenian democracy, which is widely regarded as the first known democracy in the world. The people of Athens expected well-crafted public speeches in defense of accusations. Consequently, Socrates was required to say in defense of these accusations something more than "I'm sorry fellow Athenians that you're offended by my actions."

As for the charge of impiety leveled against Socrates, another philosopher, Anaxagoras, who is sometimes lumped with other ancient Greek philosophers as one of the "pre-Socratics," had earlier been found guilty of this charge. The idea of his accusers was probably to pin Anaxagoras's views on Socrates, who if anything was the opposite of impious, as he was known, for example, to attend to religious observance without fail. But still, Socrates was not one to merely accept religious tradition without pointing out various difficulties with it—actions that would be sure to ruffle some religious feathers.

As for the charge of corrupting the youth, the motivations here were grounded more in political differences than social behavior. Socrates's circle of friends included some like Alcibiades, who had come to be regarded as political pariahs and traitors who "ruined" the country. With this charge, Socrates was arguably caught then in the crosswinds of Athenian politics. As someone who befriended folks who had strong political enemies, he then became their enemy.

My aim here is not to defend the guilt or innocence of Socrates. Nor is it to revisit the political motivations of the charges leveled against him. Many others have done these things far better than I could ever do. Rather, it is to point out something largely ignored in considerations of the birth of Western philosophy: namely, that without the accusations of Meletus, Anytus, and Lycon, and without an account of Socrates's defense against these accusations, it is quite possible that philosophy in the West might have taken quite a different course—and that he may not have become the "father" of Western philosophy. Or, positively stated: Socrates's "apology" in 399 BCE is where Western philosophy begins. Without this particular apology, Western philosophy would need to be completely rewritten.

❧

Today, our political divides are no less intense than those of Athenian Greece. The recent Brett Kavanaugh Supreme Court hearings,[11] for example, saw a country polarized by the nomination of a judge who some believe needs to stand trial like Socrates—and others think exemplifies the type of personal identity and form of conduct of those seated on our highest court.

Intensity aside, one of the differences though between Athenian democratic society and American democratic society is that whereas the Athenians reveled in debate, we generally seem to be losing the desire to defend our social and political differences.

Another difference was that in Athenian democracy at the time of Socrates's trial, there was no "judge" in our sense of the term. Rather, there were officials there to regulate the proceedings. The trial was conducted by a jury of about five hundred citizens who, ironically, were called "judges." These judges were selected by lot. So, after his three accusers presented their arguments, Socrates then presented his "apology" to a large jury of "judges." This jury had the power to determine his guilt or innocence, and to decide, if guilty, on the penalty, which in his case was a vote to condemn him to death.

While today's courtroom defenses are still often elaborate, the jury is nowhere near the five-hundred "judges" of Athenian democracy. But this is not the only "courtroom" in twenty-first century America. Social media has created another one. A powerful courtroom populated by tens of millions of people who weigh in on the behavior of those publicly—though not necessarily legally—accused.

Unlike the legal courts, which provide definitive closure on guilt or innocence by rendering a verdict, the courtrooms of social media and the Internet are much more amorphous in their verdicts.

It is here, more than any other place, that we are seeing a disturbing increase in these "neoliberal apologies."

Though there are many good examples, two recent ones suffice to illustrate well my point: the cases of John Hockenberry and Jian Ghomeshi, each of whom has been accused of sexual misconduct, and recently offered "neoliberal apologies" for their actions in major American publications.

Hockenberry was a former American news correspondent (ABC, NBC) and radio host (WNYC) who retired after being accused of sexual harassment by multiple women. In an essay entitled "Exile" recently published in *Harper's* magazine,[12] Hockenberry attempted a classic "apology" for his transgressions. However, he did so by arguing that what others call "sexual harassment" should really be considered "romance."

"Do I dare make a spirited defense of something called romance," wrote Hockenberry, "from the darkness of this exile?"

He answers his own question in the affirmative: "Not only do I dare, knowing what righteous anger is out there [about sexual harassment], I really believe I have no choice."

Though Hockenberry calls this a "defense," it is a perfect example of a "neoliberal apology." There is no effort to look at the accusations directly. Also, there is an attempt to recast them under a wholly in a different category.

I'm sorry for your righteous anger at my actions, but I didn't do anything wrong. It was just romance.

We've heard a lot about this type of "romance" of late, where the wealthy, famous, and powerful use their position as a platform for all forms of sexual misconduct.

"I am surely guilty of bad judgment," said Hockenberry. "I have learned in the hardest way the price of not understanding or caring how my actions are perceived by others."

But there is "no defense" for sexual harassment. There is "no apology" for it even if clever people like Hockenberry attempt one by trying to convince us that in the new millennium, sexual harassment and romance amount to the same thing.

163

﹖♪

The second recent case revolves around an article by Jian Ghomeshi recently published in the *New York Review of Books*.[13] Ghomeshi was a Canadian broadcaster who was fired from his job in 2014 amid accusations of sexual violence, and who stood trial on sexual assault charges two years later. Like Hockenberry, Ghomeshi has been publicly shamed for his sexual misconduct, and wrote an essay in response to the shaming.

Ghomeshi's piece, "Reflections from a Hashtag," recounts how the events surrounding his public shaming for sexual misconduct were for him "a crash course in empathy." He also talks about the suicidal depression that resulted from these events. But, like Hockenberry, what he does not discuss, are the specific actions that led to his downfall. And, like Hockenberry, he too offers a long "non-apology apology" instead.

Both essays—Hockenberry's from *Harper's* and Ghomeshi's from the *New York Review of Books*—are wrought from the same neoliberal-man cloth. The trouble with these two pieces is not just the inability of these two men to show in them that they truly understand what they did wrong and to apologize appropriately for it, but also that both of these essays were shamelessly published in major American publications once known for nuanced coverage of controversial and difficult issues.

While the editor of *Harper's* appears to be unscathed from the publication of Hockenberry's essay, the editor of the *New York Review of Books* was out of his job there *before the print edition of the article even hit the newsstands!* Released first online, the essay set off a firestorm of righteous blowback directed at the person most responsible for its publication, the *Review*'s editor, Ian Buruma.

Buruma, who had no previous editorial experience but was a frequent writer for the *Review*, took over its editorship just last year.[14] Though it is unclear whether he resigned or was fired from the publication, an interview with *Slate* revealed he simply was unable or unwilling to understand why so many believe that the essay should not have been published in the *Review*. It also revealed him to be out of touch with the general ethos of the #MeToo movement. Says Buruma,

I am not going to defend [Ghomeshi's] behavior, and I don't know if what all these women are saying is true. Perhaps it is. Perhaps it isn't. My interest in running this piece, as I said, is the point of view of somebody who has been pilloried in public opinion and what somebody like that feels about it. It was not run as a piece to exonerate him or to somehow mitigate the nature of his behavior.

But this is not how it was received by many who read it. One of the first jobs of an editor is to have a sense of their audience. Through the publication of Ghomeshi's essay, Buruma revealed himself to be largely out of touch with his audience as it was and is read as an exoneration of the sexual misconduct of Ghomeshi. This is particularly apparent as he makes no effort in it to apologize for his actions.

What is even more remarkable here than the "neoliberal apologies" of Ghomeshi and Hockenberry is that both essays appeared in the same week. It is like editorial myopia struck these two esteemed publications simultaneously. Publishing the empty apologies of these men is hopefully though not a prelude to more of the same.

The Kevin Spacey's, Bill Cosby's, and Harvey Weinstein's of the world should not be given a platform to whine about their public shamings and falls from grace. We've already heard and seen enough from their likes. It is time now to hear from others. And if publications like *Harper's*, the *New York Review of Books*, and the *New Yorker* don't understand this, then we too don't need to listen to them.

ॐ

The ugly events coming to light through the #MeToo movement affords our society the opportunity to learn again how to apologize.

By publishing the empty apologies of those justly trampled underfoot by public outcry in support of the victims of their sexual misconduct, major publications like *Harper's* and the *New York Review of Books* are themselves contributing to the problem instead of trying to help resolve it.

The only explanation for publishing these pieces is that it is an effort to cash in on the celebrity status of the perpetrators. But their efforts to increase their bottom lines reveal a complete *disregard for the interests of those at whose expense these apologies come.* To provide more balanced reporting, they need to include statements from the accusers; to avoid the perception that they are profiting from publishing these "non-apology apologies," they should consider donating a portion of the proceeds from the sale of these issues to an appropriate non-profit dedicated to remediating sexual misconduct.

The now common, all-too-common, neoliberal apology completely disregards the welfare of others. It gives famous and powerful public figures a statement behind which they may hide but not escape from public judgment.

At the heart of Socratic philosophy is the idea that the unexamined life is not worth living. This examination comes in the form of questions that we continuously pose to ourselves throughout our lives. Key among those questions are three that Kurt Cobain posed in the lyrics to his classic song, "All Apologies":

> *What else should I be? .... What else could I say? .... What else could I write?*

The philosophical and democratic spirit lives in our society as long as we continue to ask questions like these. It dies when our questioning stops and our apologies become non-apologies.

Let's hope that this new genre of writing, the neoliberal apology, is a short-lived one.

20 | FREETHINKERS AND HERETICS

They unanimously agreed to hire him. He accepted their invitation.

The nineteen board members in attendance (of a total of twenty-two members) agreed to appoint one of the world's most eminent philosophers to a position at their college. The appointment would be for seventeen months and would begin in one year. Two senior faculty members were retiring. Replacing one with a revered scholar, a living legend, must have felt like an easy decision.

"I know that your acceptance of this appointment will add luster to the name and achievement of the department," wrote Ordway Tead, chairman of the board, "and that it will deepen and extend the interest of the college in the philosophic basis of human living."

When he accepted the new appointment, Bertrand Russell was teaching at the University of California. The fall before he was to join the City College of New York's philosophy department, he was scheduled to give the William James Lectures at Harvard University. At the City College of New York, he was only scheduled to teach three courses: one on the philosophical foundations of mathematics; a second on the relationship between logic to science, mathematics, and philosophy; and a third on the "relations of pure to applied sciences and the reciprocal influence of metaphysics and scientific theories."

At 67 years of age, though Russell's research career in mathematical philosophy was well behind him and had arguably reached its zenith in the first two decades of the century with the publication of *The Principles of Mathematics* in 1903, and later the co-writing of the three volume *Principia Mathematica* (1910-1913) with Alfred North Whitehead, there was probably no one more qualified in the world to fulfill this teaching assignment at CCNY.

Yet within days of his appointment, a chorus of public opposition formed—one that had not been seen in American higher education and which to this day remains unequalled.

Bishop Manning of the Protestant Episcopal Church wrote a letter to the New York newspapers denouncing Russell's appointment. "What is to be said of colleges and universities which hold up before our youth as a responsible teacher of philosophy," wrote the Bishop, "a man who is a recognized propagandist against both religion and morality, and who specifically defends adultery?"

"Can anyone who cares for the welfare of our country," he added, "be willing to see such teaching disseminated with the countenance of our colleges and universities?"

Others soon joined the bandwagon of vilification and moral outrage at his appointment. Russell was described variously as a "professor of paganism" and "the philosophical anarchist and moral nihilist of Great Britain," whose appointment to a position at CCNY was a "brutal, insulting shock to old New Yorkers and all real Americans."

The Borough President of Queens, George V. Harvey went so far as to say that if the college did not annul the appointment, he would move to eliminate the entire appropriation allotted to the upkeep of the New York City municipal colleges, which in 1941 amounted to 7.5 million dollars. Harvey announced that "the colleges would either be godly colleges, American colleges, or they would be closed."

When the Board failed, in spite of increasing public pressure, to annul Russell's appointment to City College, a taxpayer's suit was filed with the New York Supreme Court on the grounds that he was an alien and an advocate of sexual immorality. Mrs. Jean Kay of Brooklyn filed the suit on behalf of her daughter, Gloria. She feared what might happen to her daughter if she took one of Russell's courses at City College—even though at the time only men could take day-session courses in the liberal arts at City College.

Her lawyer, Joseph Goldstein, described Russell's works in his brief as "lecherous, libidinous, lustful, venerous, erotomaniac, aphrodisiac, irreverent, narrow-minded, untruthful, and bereft of moral fiber." He also said that Russell "conducted a nudist colony in England. His children paraded nude. He and his wife have paraded nude in public. This man who is now about seventy has gone in for salacious poetry. Russell winks at homosexuality. I'd go further and say he approves of it." Leaving no slander and insult unsaid, Goldstein concludes:

> He is not a philosopher in the accepted meaning of the word; not a lover of wisdom . . . he is a sophist; practices sophism; that by cunning contrivances, tricks and devices and by mere quibbling, he puts forth fallacious arguments

and arguments that are not supported by sound reasoning; and he draws inferences which are not justly deduced from a sound premise; that all his alleged doctrines which he calls philosophy are just cheap, tawdry, worn-out, patched-up fetishes and propositions, devised for the purpose of misleading people.

Responding to the only legally relevant point in the brief, the point that an alien could not be appointed to a post at City College, the lawyer for the Board of Higher Education asked that the case be dismissed. The presiding judge however denied this request and focused instead on the books introduced to the court by Goldstein: *What I Believe* (1925), *Education and the Good Life* (1926), *Marriage and Morals* (1929), and *Education and the Modern World* (1932).

Justice McGeehan's ruling revoked Lord Russell's appointment, describing it as "an insult to the people of the City of New York." According to him, the Board "in effect established a chair of indecency," and "acted arbitrarily, capriciously, and in direct violation of the public health, safety, and the morals of the people and of the petitioner's rights." Mayor La Guardia closed off all hope that Russell would be reappointed by eliminating the budget appropriation for his lectureship. The philosopher who McGeehan said was "not fit to teach in any of the schools of this land" went on to deliver the William James Lectures at Harvard and the Machette Lectures at Columbia University. He also taught a couple of years for the Barnes Foundation in Pennsylvania. In England, he was later awarded the Order of Merit by King George VI, and in 1950, he received the Nobel Prize for Literature.

Over the course of just over a month—his appointment was announced on February 24, 1940 and Judge McGeehan's ruling was on March 30—America ridiculed, tried, and convicted its modern day Socrates. Aside from the fact that Russell was not scheduled to teach courses on ethics and social and political philosophy, and would only have taught male students at City College at the time, he was found guilty of *potentially* corrupting the youth of New York City.

In 1957, New York University philosophy professor Paul Edwards published an edited volume of Russell's writing that collected many of the works by him that were allegedly a "violation of the public

169

health, safety, and the morals of the people." Edwards, who had also taught philosophy at City College, published the book at a time when Russell's student, Ludwig Wittgenstein, was surpassing his teacher in terms of influence in the philosophy world, particularly after the posthumous publication of his *Philosophical Investigations* in 1953.

Edwards used the occasion to defend Russell against the accusations made against him in 1940. In his preface to the volume, Russell repeats some of the convictions that put him at odds with the New Yorkers. "I think that all the great religions of the world— Buddhism, Hinduism, Christianity, Islam, and Communism—both untrue and harmful," comments Russell. "It is evident as a matter of logic that, since they disagree, not more than one of them can be true," states the philosopher. "With very few exceptions, the religion which a man accepts is that of the community in which he lives, which makes it obvious that the influence of environment is what has led him to accept the religion in question."

Examples of the harms wrought by religions are the

> Catholic condemnation of birth control, if it could prevail, would make the mitigation of poverty and the abolition of war impossible. The Hindu beliefs that the cow is a sacred animal and that it is wicked for widows to remarry cause quite needless suffering. The Communist belief in the dictatorship of a minority of True Believers has produced a whole crop of abominations.

Russell advocated forming a "habit of basing convictions upon evidence, and of giving to them only that degree of certainty which the evidence warrants." This habit, he says, if generalized, would "cure most of the ills from which the world is suffering." "The world," he says, "needs open hearts and open minds, and it is not through rigid systems, whether old or new, that these can be derived." This advice here is as sound and needed today as it was 60 years ago when he wrote it.

The lead essay in the Edwards volume is one that Russell originally delivered as a lecture at Battersea Town Hall under the auspices of the South London Branch of the National Secular Society of England. The title of the lecture, "Why I Am Not a Christian: An Examination of the God-Idea and Christianity," delivered on March

6, 1927, takes up many of the topics that fueled opposition to Russell's appointment at City College. However, based on his comments in the preface to the Edwards volume, the "Christian" in the title could have been equally substituted with "Buddhist," "Hindu," "Muslim," or "Communist" and would have been equally heretical to their respective communities. Nonetheless, to present these ideas to a Christian audience or community is to invite its ire—and this is just what Russell wanted. For that matter, much of his work on religion and morality contained a level of antagonism achieved in the last century only by a small group of popular writers.

Edwards used the title of Russell's essay for his edited collection. *Why I Am Not a Christian and Other Essays on Religion and Related Subjects*, the full title of the 1957 collection, like the title of the essay itself, leaves no doubt where Russell stands in terms of Christianity. Variations on this form of title existed before Russell's lecture (for example, Karel Čapek published an essay entitled "Why I Am Not a Communist" in 1924) and continue to the present (for example, Kancha Ilaiah's *Why I Am Not a Hindu* [1996] and Ibn Warraq, *Why I Am Not a Muslim* [1995]) because it is a powerful and provocative one given the right object of first-person negation.

But the first publication of this essay though was not in the Edwards volume or even in one of Russell's many books, but rather as a booklet. In April of 1927, Watt & Company of London reproduced it in booklet form for the Rationalist Press Association Limited. Five thousand copies were printed on thick, cream-colored, wove paper, which was sewn and glued to a grey paper wrapper. Presumably to protect the Rationalist Press and Watt & Company from possible recrimination, the booklet included the statement, "It should be added that the author alone is responsible for the political and other opinions expressed."

As word of the lecture spread, translation and reprinting followed. It was translated into Czech in 1928, French in 1929, and Polish and German in 1932. Later it appeared in Afrikaans in 1955, Finish in 1957, Russian in 1958, Russian/Armenian and Hungarian in 1960, and Lithuanian in 1965.

Its first publication in the United States though was in the *Haldeman-Julius Quarterly* in 1928. The quarterly, then in its second year of publication, devoted six pages in its July/August/September issue to reprinting Russell's lecture in its entirety.

171

Given its popularity in Britain—the publishers ended up producing six impressions of it amounting to 19,000 copies total in 1927 and 1928 alone—it should be no surprise that the following year, Haldeman-Julius Company would also decide to publish it in the United States as a booklet.

This American publishing company specialized in provocative and controversial writing. Their booklets, first published in 1919 as the New Appeal's "Pocket Series," came to be known (after the publication of 210 titles) as the Little Blue Books. Printed on poor quality, thin wove paper, which was stapled twice in the center to a soft blue paper cover with black print, these small books would, according to R. Alton Lee, "revolutionize the book-publishing industry."

In *Publisher for the Masses: Emanuel Haldeman-Julius* (2017), his study of their general editor and publisher, Lee contends Haldeman-Julius "became the greatest publisher in world history" because he sold 500 million copies of the 2,580 titles that his press published. According to Lee, this "was second only to the U.S. Government Printing Office" in terms of quantity of publications.

The books, which sold for as little as a nickel, were aimed at "Mr. Average Man." While some were simply reprints of the shorter classics of world literature including the plays of Shakespeare, many others rivaled Russell's volume in terms of being a "violation of the public health, safety, and the morals of the people." By the time Russell's *Why I Am Not a Christian* was published in 1929 as Little Blue Book No. 1372— a 32 page booklet with a price-tag of 5 cents—the following titles were already in print and had sold very well: *Women's Sexual Life* (97,000 copies sold), *Homosexual Life* (54,500), *Modern Aspects of Birth Control* (73,000 copies sold in spite of the fact that it was *illegal* to publish or distribute contraceptive material), *Catholicism and Sex* (65,000), *Prostitution in the Modern World* (129,500), *Why I Believe in Companionate Marriage* (64,000 copies and written by Emanuel's wife, Marcet Haldeman-Julius), *Facts about Venereal Disease* (41,500), *Love Letters of a Portuguese Nun* (46,000), *Sex Obsessions of Saints and Mystics* (35,000) and *What Can a Free Man Worship?* (24,000, also written by Russell).

But in addition to the sex, religion, marriage, and love books, there were also "How to" Little Blue Books on just about anything one could imagine as well as titles on many areas of common knowledge. And these too sold well.

Emanuel was a socialist, a freethinker, and like Russell, a heretic. And, unlike Russell's first British publisher, his first American publisher openly embraced Russell's opinions in *Why I Am Not a Christian*, prefacing their publication in 1929 with the statement: "It should be added that the editor [Emanuel Haldeman-Julius] is willing to share full responsibility with the Hon. Bertrand Russell in that he is in accord with the political and other opinions expressed."

In addition to the Little Blue Books, Emanuel also published at different points a weekly, a quarterly, and a monthly, and often used them to raise funds for his little books. In 1923, he was already looking to print 80,000 books per day in his facilities, and relished being called "The Henry Ford of Literature."

Given the negative public reaction to Russell's appointment to a position at City College, and the nature of much of the material published by the Haldeman-Julius Company, it might not be surprising that the company and its presses were not located in New York City. However, given that New York City was and is the publishing industry capital of the United States, it *is* somewhat shocking that "the greatest publisher in world history" *was not* located in the city. But rather in a tiny town of 2,000, which Emanuel moved to *from* New York City.

In 1915, Louis Kopelin, one of his former employers, offered Emanuel a position as an editorial assistant for *Appeal to Reason*, the leading socialist newspaper in the world with a circulation of 750,000.

It was located in Girard, Kansas.

Emanuel Haldeman-Julius made publishing history from a tiny town in Kansas where he lived, wrote, and published until his death in 1951.

According to R. Alton Lee, residents of Girard never bothered him about the content of his newspaper or little blue books. And for the most part, he distributed them throughout the world with very little interference from the U.S. Post Office—and none from the post office in Girard.

These books, written by freethinkers and heretics, were purchased and read by millions and millions of people with nary any legal issues. However, when a college in New York City offered a post to a professor who published several volumes for the press, the moral wrath of residents of the publishing capital of the world came down upon him for many of the same opinions upon which Emanuel Haldeman-Julius made publishing history.

It should be noted that when the Russell kerfuffle hit NYC in 1940, a second American edition of his famous essay was published by the Freethought Press Association located on 34th Street in New York, NY. More a pamphlet than a booklet, with a trim size of 5 x 7½ inches, its 24 pages seem in retrospect like a desperate publishing afterthought given that Little Blue Book No. 1372 had been in U.S. circulation now for over a decade.

In our time of religious fanaticism and denial of many beliefs in spite of the preponderance of evidence in their favor, a glance back to the freethinkers and heretics of the last century can provide a measure of courage for contemporary writers and publishers pursuing their own "cures for the ills of the world."

"The world needs open hearts and open minds" because closed ones serve to intensify and perpetuate war and suffering worldwide.

Where are our generation's Little Blue Books? Who today is writing and publishing them?

21 | THE GENEROUS PROFESSOR

Academe is not particularly known for its generosity. While we encourage faculty to teach, research, and serve their university, they are not required to fulfill any of these tasks with "generosity." Excellence in teaching is usually determined by how well class material has been prepared and taught, not by the generosity of the professor. Moreover, professors who are characterized as generous are often the ones who routinely do things like raise borderline student grades, drop exams and assignments, and make exceptions for deadlines—a form of generosity that often has a negative ripple effect on colleagues who play by the rules and do not deviate from the requirements of their syllabus.

In terms of research, being generous often amounts to looking for every possible way to find merit in the research of others. A student paper that is bad might be read generously by a professor as "not so bad" or even "pretty good" so as to not discourage a student in their future academic endeavors. But here too there is the potential for a negative ripple effect on colleagues who then get students who have a falsely-inflated sense of their research capabilities and expect a similar generous response to their work. The generosity of our faint praise of poor research thus damns both the student and professor.

Finally, in terms of service, the characteristic of generosity is often afforded the colleague who agrees to serve on every committee for which they are asked. Unlike generosity in teaching and research, which more often than not has a negative ripple effect with ones colleagues (for example, the expectation of flexibility in grading and deadlines), service generosity has less of a negative ripple effect as it lightens the service demands of ones colleagues unless, of course, these are service tasks that one wants or needs but have been denied because of the generous professor.

In short, generosity is something that we often see in academe though its consequences are not always good or desirable ones. To be tagged as the "generous professor" is often to be marked as a colleague who makes life harder on one's colleagues. Like a good-cop/bad-cop routine, the generous professor (viz., the good cop) bends the rules for their students thereby making them happy, whereas the ungenerous professor (viz., the bad cop) who refuses to raise a grade or faintly praise a piece of bad writing is the recipient of student anger and complaints.

The topic of generosity then in academe is an interesting one because of the way it can turn a virtue into a vice. The question of its role in the university is therefore a significant one if generosity is something that we want our students to both value and practice in society after graduation. No one would argue that generous neighbors are a bad thing. However, just on the basis of the brief exercise above, generous professors are another matter entirely.

In *Generous Thinking: A Radical Approach to Saving the University*, Kathleen Fitzpatrick argues that doubling-down on generosity in academe is one way to save the university.[15] She views her approach as "radical" because foregrounding a positive role for generosity in the university goes against much of its current operating system. This operating system or "paradigm" as she calls it involves a continuous push for increasing levels of university prestige through competition. Universities are continuously comparing their achievements in not only teaching, research, and service, but also in areas such as fundraising, athletics, and job placement in a race to the top. Every institution of higher education in America measures itself relative to those on top or most highly ranked. Moreover, amidst all this competition and comparison, no one seems to be listening to anyone else both within the academy and outside of it. Fitzpatrick argues that we just need to slow everything down and focus on listening to the opinions of others.

For Fitzpatrick, one of the major problems with the academy today is that it does not connect well with the public. She believes that even if we in the academy disagree with folks in the public, we still need to not just listen to them, but to listen to them *generously*. Generous listening is for her "the heart of generosity" and "the necessary ground for generous thinking." "Generous listening," in the words of Krista Tippett from her book *Becoming Wise: An Inquiry into the Mystery and Art of Living* (2016), which Fitzpatrick quotes, "is powered by curiosity, a virtue we can invite and nurture in ourselves to render it instructive. It involves a kind of vulnerability—a willingness to be surprised, to let go of assumptions and take in ambiguity. The listener wants to understand the humanity behind the words of the other, and patiently summons one's own best self and one's own best words and questions." By publicly practicing generous listening, members of the academy have the best chance to understand the arguments or beliefs of those outside of the academy, particularly those who are opposed to providing state funds for its support and believe that the university should be run like a private corporation. Generous listening thus enables the generous thinking that will work to create a "shared vocabulary" that will help bridge the interests of the university community with the broader public community. "As a community," writes Fitzpatrick, "the university, those who work within it, and those who care about it have obligations to work toward that more generous, more ethical engagement, and that work must begin with listening, with attention."

While there is a lot of talk of ethical engagement with others, Fitzpatrick avoids a full out defense of an ethics of generosity opting instead to champion elements of Kwame Anthony Appiah's cosmopolitanism, Nell Noddings's caring, and Bill Readings's obligation and "commitment to dissensus—the willingness to dwell in an ongoing disagreement and dialogue rather than forcing a false and oppressive consensus." This opportunity must be left to others though Fitzpatrick calling the question of a possible transformative role for generosity in the university to come—the university that moves beyond the status quo of neoliberal academe—is an interesting one. Though she does not mention the ethics of Emmanuel Levinas in her book its consideration could carry some weight in her project. For Levinas, the provider of true generosity does not expect reciprocity in return from its beneficiary and considers all deserving of it. No one is more or less deserving of generosity, rather the entire community is its object. For Levinas, this is possible through an unconditional openness to the Other. However, such an unconditional openness to the Other comes with a cost to our own identity: it calls it into question.

While Levinas squares well with the ideas espoused for generosity in terms of listening and thinking by Fitzpatrick its form of relationship with the Other is problematic if practiced in neoliberal academe. Why? Because neoliberal academe flourishes in the context

177

of docile subjectivity. Thus, to move beyond neoliberal academe, a world build upon competition, prestige, and the market, we need to also move beyond docile subjects. I have argued this point at length in *Corporate Humanities in Higher Education* (2013) though have not considered a role for generosity in our quest to fight back against the tyranny of the neoliberal university. At first pass though, neither the work of Readings, Noddings, Appiah, or Levinas on generosity is going to allow for a form of academic agency sufficiently strong to resist the docile subject-formation of neoliberal academe. In my own estimation, the ethics of Michel Foucault and Jean-François Lyotard, particularly the latter's notion of paralogy, offers our best hope for the formation of a new university that is not doomed to repeat the past (viz., the modern university) and not committed to making the mistakes of the present (viz., the neoliberal university). This requires not only a complete reconsideration of the economic, academic, and professional model of the modern educational system, but also must be approached with a different *vision*—one which, I argue, should be grounded more on a "negative dialogics" (viz., one which encourages systemic dissent and foregrounds epistemological instabilities and heterogeneous identities) than a "positive dialogics" (viz., one which encourages systemic consensus, and foregrounds epistemological stabilities and homogeneous identities). In the end, this paralogical vision will not only help the academy to get beyond the hegemonic and repressive order of the neoliberal university, but also will hasten the formation of the nonhegemonic, progressive *dis*order of the university to come, that is, the postmodern university.

This, of course, is not the way forward for Fitzpatrick. The negative dialogics of progressive educational theorists such as Paulo Freire, Henry Giroux, and Kenneth Saltman, in addition to the poststructuralist theory of Foucault, Lyotard, and Derrida are nowhere to be found in this book. Nor is there a strong role for critique in saving the university. Rather, the aims of generous listening and thought are more representative of a "positive dialogics," one that encourages systemic consensus through listening and the creation of shared vocabularies, epistemological stabilities, and homogeneous identities. These positive dialogics are directly associated in her chapter on "Reading Together" with the postcritique of Rita Felski who is one of a handful of scholars whose work she mentions and uses more than once or twice. The rub though for Fitzpatrick is that while she says that "I do not think that critique per se is the problem," she nevertheless does not call upon any of its masters, e.g., Freud, Marx, Nietzsche, Foucault, Lyotard, Derrida, Freire, and Giroux, in her analysis of the ills of the university today. Moreover, while praising throughout the volume the post-critical contributions of Felski, Fitzpatrick nevertheless wants to "reorient" Felski's postcritique project "to focus not on the critical as the dominant mood of our work but instead the competitive, the costs of which are astronomical, not only to each individual scholar in setting the course toward stress-related burnout, but to scholars collectively in undermining our ability to understand ourselves as a community, one capable of disagreeing profoundly and yet still coming together in solidarity to argue for our collective interests." But isn't "the competitive" the engine of neoliberalism and that which critique seeks to undermine? So why not focus on critique as a way to overcome neoliberal academe instead of advocating postcritical scholarship that aligns well with the interests of the neoliberal academic project?

The difference between positive and negative dialogics though cut even deeper. For Jürgen Habermas, the goal of dialogue is consensus. Generous listening and thought through dialogue has the same goal: a consensus between the perspectives of the academy and the voices of the public. This positive dialogics could not be further from the negative dialogics of Lyotard where "consensus," as he says in *The Postmodern Condition* (1984), "is only a particular state of discussion, not its end." While Lyotard champions dialogue it is not for its ability for us to reach consensus and stability, but rather dissent and instability, that is to say, paralogy. Where then does generosity fit into a paralogical approach to saving the university? The answer is perhaps found in Derrida's notion of the gift—one that turns Levinas's generosity without reciprocity into an impossibility. For Derrida, a soon as the receiver of a gift recognizes it as a gift, the received becomes indebted to the giver. The obligation of the receiver to provide a gift in return collapses this alleged act of generosity into a form of economic exchange. Consequently, for Derrida a gift is only possible if the giver and the receiver do not recognize that an exchange has taken place. It is in similar fashion I would argue that generosity needs to function in the neoliberal academy to overcome or deconstruct its neoliberal economic foundations. True generosity

179

along these lines would be just as impossible as Derrida's gift. And just as there is no such thing as a gift for Derrida, so too would there be no such thing as generosity—whether in the form of generous listening, thinking, or giving.

Of course much more would need to be said to build a compelling case for a negative dialogics of generosity. However, given the genealogy of generosity, it seems worth pursuing if we want to locate a sense of generosity not rooted in economic exchange. Just a brief consideration of the etymology of generosity should establish this: the Latin root of the English word generosity means "of noble birth." In fact, the most common use of "generous" through the sixteenth century is in connection to noble birth. Thus, to be generous was to belong to the nobility. While the modern usage associates it more with a virtue of individuals, it is difficult to shake its foundations in economic exchange when corporations and governments can be characterized by generosity as much as individuals including professors.

Back now to our "generous" professors who exhibit this characteristic in their teaching, research, and service. In the context of the neoliberal university, these acts or practices of generosity must be seen as forms of economic exchange, that is, acts whose ultimate ground is the reciprocity of the financial compensation of the university. Professors generally expect to be compensated at some level for their teaching, research, and service. Therefore there is *impossibility* in a Derridean sense in characterizing their actions as generous even if the object of their generosity is an increased level of attention to the other through more listening or a pronounced effort to give every belief and argument as much thought and attention as is humanly possible, especially when one finds it to be prima facie wrongheaded.

In short, to advocate for the increased practice of generosity within the context of the neoliberal academy only serves to extend further its life cycle—a characteristic it fittingly shares with postcritique. Still, for positive dialogicians such as Fitzpatrick, the hope remains that through generous listening and thinking we can reach consensus and a shared vocabulary with a public that increasingly does not understand the value of what we do or why they should support it. And here she is not alone in this belief. There is an extensive literature built on saving higher education through acts of docile subjectivity and Fitzpatrick uses it well to build her case for generous thinking. Nevertheless, I believe that the negative dialogics of Freire, Foucault, Giroux, Lyotard, and Derrida are a more effective approach to saving the university. I agree with Fitzpatrick that listening and thinking are important to this task but fundamentally disagree with her on the potential of generosity to help us move beyond the neoliberal university.

22 | THE PROFIT OF THE HUMANITIES

Democratic education is under siege and could very well vanish from the American educational system. "Thirsty for national profit, nations, and their systems of education," writes Martha Nussbaum in *Not for Profit: Why Democracy Needs the Humanities*, "are heedlessly discarding skills that are needed to keep democracies alive."[16] "If this trend continues, nations all over the world will soon be producing generations of useful machines, rather than complete citizens who can think for themselves, criticize tradition, and understand the significance of another person's sufferings and achievements," continues Nussbaum. "The future of world's democracies hangs in the balance."

Not for Profit presents a passionate case for systems of education that result in "a more inclusive type of citizenship"—rather than ones solely focused on profit-making. For Nussbaum, the humanities and the arts are the place where students acquire the "skills" necessary to keep democracies alive and become complete citizens—rather than "useful machines." If we continue to "ask our schools to turn out useful profit-makers rather than thoughtful citizens," our world will become one comprised of "technically trained people who do not know how to criticize authority, useful profit-makers with obtuse imaginations." According to Nussbaum, "greedy obtuseness" and "technically trained docility" "threaten the very life of democracy itself" and "impede the creation of a decent world culture."

From a wide angle, Nussbaum presents a compelling case for the importance of the humanities to the development of democratic culture. Critical thinking and reflection provide citizens with the capacity to see beyond local problems and loyalties and "imagine sympathetically the predicament of another person." Imagination and thought enriches our relationships with others and "makes us human." However, the single-minded quest for economic growth and financial profit tends to abandon these democratic values, particularly in times of severe economic crisis. As a result, democratic education gives way to education for profit in times of financial crisis.

"Distracted by the pursuit of wealth," comments Nussbaum, "we increasingly ask our schools to turn out useful profit-makers rather than thoughtful citizens." Economic strains only exacerbate this situation and put pressure on institutions to abandon the liberal arts model of university education. This model, which flourishes in the United States and is unlike that of just about every other nation in the world, gives students the freedom to study a wide range of courses during the first two years of their university education. Rather than focusing on studying a single subject, students educated in the liberal arts model of education take an array of courses spanning the arts and sciences. The liberal arts model challenges "the mind to become active, competent, and thoughtfully critical in a complex world" rather than encouraging students to passively assimilate "facts and cultural traditions." The result is a model of education that produces "informed, independent, and sympathetic democratic citizens."

To this point, Nussbaum's argument for the importance of the humanities to democratic citizenship is relatively uncontroversial. Nussbaum draws heavily on the educational philosophies of John Dewey and Rabindranath Tagore to make her case, and in the process demonstrates many of the similarities between their positions. For admirers of Dewey's educational philosophy unfamiliar with the work of Tagore, her comparisons will be interesting. In addition, comparing highly influential Indian and American educational philosophies in support of liberal arts education gives her general argument a more global feel, and makes her sub-arguments such as those against educational practices that merely "teach to the test" and those that advocate passive memorization (over active learning) even more compelling. Nonetheless, Nussbaum's case against education for profit somehow still takes a wrong turn.

Instead of simply arguing that active learning in the humanities is necessary to democratic education, Nussbaum also adds that it leads to economic growth—and financial profit. A "flourishing economy," writes Nussbaum, "requires the same skills that support citizenship." In her opinion, those who believe that passive pedagogies, technical training, and the elimination of the humanities curriculum lead to economic growth are mistaken. While it may not look like programs in the arts and humanities lead to economic growth, argues Nussbaum, they do. So how?

Education in the arts and humanities cultivate and develop sympathy. For Nussbaum, sympathy is necessary for economic development that values equality. Comments Nussbaum, "a cultivated and developed sympathy is a particularly dangerous enemy of obtuseness, and moral obtuseness is necessary to carry out programs of economic development that ignore inequality." Paraphrasing Tagore, Nussbaum writes "aggressive nationalism needs to blunt the moral conscience, so it needs people who do not recognize the individual, who speak group-speak, who behave, and see the world, like docile bureaucrats." Nussbaum's point here is that if equality and concern for the lives of others are important, then we will favor a form of economic development that promotes them.

For Nussbaum, the arts and humanities are where we gain the ability to not only "think well about political issues affecting the nation," but also "to recognize fellow citizens as people with equal rights, even though they may be different in race, religion, gender, and sexuality: to look at them with respect, as ends, not just as tools to be manipulated for one's own profit." As such, those who promote educational models based on the acquisition of highly applied skills as the optimal means toward profit making and economic growth "have adopted an impoverished conception of what is required to meet their own goal." For Nussbaum, critical thinking and global awareness are just as important to the future of democracies—as they are to the promotion of education for profit.

For many, though, bridging an education for democracy with one for profit is an exercise in futility. The former leads to the advocacy of public goods such as health, education, equality, and liberty; the latter though, which in its neoliberal form, promotes the unfettered flow of the global market and economic growth as the source of value, decimates public goods such as health, education, equality, and liberty. In fact, Nussbaum even notes that empirical studies have shown these public goods are "very poorly correlated with economic growth." For example, old South Africa under apartheid used to be at the top of the economic development indices even though it featured "staggering distributional inequalities, the brutal apartheid regime, and the health and educational deficiencies that went with it." In addition, contemporary China may be enjoying economic growth, but you would not be able to predict this from its record on political liberty.

"So," remarks Nussbaum, "producing economic growth does not mean producing democracy."

One way to describe the blind spot in Nussbaum's position is its total omission of any discussion of how *neoliberalism* has decimated higher education and democratic values. In fact, not only is the term not mentioned in the book, there is very little acknowledgement as to the role of the market in determining value and reshaping educational practice. While it may be true that liberal arts education can produce both a democratic culture and economic development, students now tend to look to higher education as a means to increase their profit-making capacities rather than their political ones. And universities that are focused on promoting democratic culture rather than profitable jobs for their graduates are becoming more the exception than the norm.

If Nussbaum's argument is the best that liberal humanism can give to the neoliberal onslaught, then liberal education in America should be worried. The days of arguing that the arts and the humanities should be supported because they produce good citizens have been swept away by the tsunami of global capital. Moreover, trying to beat neoliberal education at the "profit" game is a losing endeavor. While Nussbaum presents a compelling case why democracy needs the humanities, she does not present a convincing case as to how public goods such as health, education, equality, and liberty can be protected in the age of neoliberalism. Thirty years ago, at the height of the age of multiculturalism, Nussbaum's arguments might have held more sway than they do today. However, by trying to argue that the humanities is good both for democracy *and* the bottom-line, Nussbaum has fails to address the major challenge of the day: namely, why be a liberal humanist when neoliberalism appears to have a much more profitable upside? Nussbaum opens the door for this criticism by trying to argue *for profit* in a book entitled *Not for Profit*.

23 | THIS HUMANITIES WHICH IS NOT ONE

It is old news that the humanities are in peril. It is also well known that their crisis is not just going to go away on its own—even though some humanists seem to act as though this were the case. In fact, there is every reason to believe that neoliberal educational practices and the growth of the corporate university are only going to deepen the problems facing the humanities. Declining numbers of majors, reductions in financial support, and a general lack of understanding of the nature and value of the humanities are opening the door to a more vocationally-centered vision of higher education. In a political economy and academic environment wherein educational values are determined by market-share, majors and courses that cannot be directly connected to marketable skills and job attainment are regarded as expendable. As a result, the humanities are losing students and energy at an alarming rate—and are in need of reprieve, if not renewal.

So what is going to provide the reprieve? Where will the renewal come from? What is going to end the decline? Humanities scholars have been very good at pointing fingers at others for their woes, but have been hard pressed to provide convincing arguments in support of humanities education. In particular, they have had difficulty making a case for the humanities that is convincing not only to those inside the humanities, but also to those *outside* of the humanities; credible to those informed about the humanities as well as to those *uniformed* about them; persuasive to those sympathetic to the humanities as well as to those *hostile* to them.

Martha Nussbaum's arguments in *Not for Profit* typify the difficulties facing the liberal humanist response to the problems facing the humanities. Again, though they present strong arguments for the role of the humanities in democracy, they are not as effective in making the case that the humanities necessarily serve the ends of neoliberal capital. The liberal humanist ideal of the public good is set aside under neoliberalism and consequently, education, equality, liberty, and other common goods are eroded. Though it may be pragmatic to argue as Nussbaum does that the humanities are good for democracy *and* the bottom-line, this argument fails to address why one would want to make this form of liberal humanist argument when the path of the neoliberal is a much more profitable one.

In many ways, Nussbaum's book is the perfect foil for Toby Miller's intervention into the crisis in the humanities debate. If Nussbaum's project can be described as a taking the high road in defending the humanities, then Miller's *Blow Up the Humanities* might be described as taking the *low road*.[17] Miller begins his book by claiming that the humanities in the United States are not what most think they are, namely, a unified, monological entity. Rather, for Miller, the humanities are radically divided.

On the one hand, there is "the humanities of fancy private universities, where the bourgeoisie and its favored subalterns are tutored in finishing school"; on the other hand, there "is the humanities of everyday state schools, which focus more on job prospects." The former he terms "Humanities One," and the latter "Humanities Two." His aim is both to establish the "two humanities" distinction—one that is, by the way, directly inspired by C. P. Snow's famous "two cultures" distinction—and then to blow it up. In its place, Miller seeks the reunification of the humanities, that is, a type of merger between Humanities One and Humanities Two. But before we turn to what a reunified humanities looks like, let's dwell a bit on how and why Miller thinks the humanities today are radically divided.

For some, it might have been enough to leave the division between the two humanities as one relative to institutional prestige. For example, it is not difficult to imagine that studying social and political philosophy with John Rawls at Harvard University or Martha Nussbaum at the University of Chicago would be a greatly different educational experience than studying it with an overworked and underpaid philosopher at a state school. Or, that studying the humanities at a "fancy private university" would be more academically oriented (e.g., aimed at pursuing an academic career in the humanities) and that studying them at an "everyday state school" would be more vocationally oriented (e.g. aimed at using the humanities to acquire job skills). But this is *not* what Miller does.

Rather, after dividing the humanities into "Humanities One" and "Humanities Two," he then distributes the disciplines in the humanities between them. Humanities One is assigned "literature, history, and philosophy" and Humanities Two is assigned "communication and media studies." Fittingly, Humanities One is the humanities of Nussbaum, the Ernst Freund Distinguished Service Professor of Law and Ethics in the Philosophy Department, Law School, and Divinity School at the University of Chicago, and Humanities Two is the humanities of Miller, the Distinguished Professor of Media and Cultural Studies at the University of California, Riverside. The former, a fancy private university; the latter, an everyday state school.

Though Miller concedes that the disciplinary assignments of Humanities One and Humanities Two are "far from absolute," he contends that they are "heuristically and statistically persuasive." His evidence here comes from two different statistical streams: the first shows that "[t]he vast growth in higher education from the 1970s has taken place among the lower middle and working classes," which tend to "enroll in state schools that are more vocational than private ones"; the second shows that whereas English, foreign language, philosophy, and history majors have declined since the 1970s, communication and media studies majors have increased. Regarding the latter, one of the more surprising statistics cited by Miller is that "[b]etween 1970 and 2005, business enrollments increased by 176 percent," whereas during the same period communication and media studies increased by a jaw-dropping 616 percent.

While it is possible to pick holes in Miller's distinctions and evidence, they still provide an intriguing point of entry into current debates concerning the humanities. Namely, Miller's "two humanities" distinction calls for us now to ask in humanities crisis discourse *which* or *whose* "humanities" is being referenced. Moreover, if nothing else, Miller has shown that at least a sub-section of the disciplines in the humanities are *not* in peril. As such, by pointing out that students are attracted to communication and media studies in rapidly growing numbers, Miller in effect gives the humanities in a time of crisis a new base upon which to build support. The problem with this though— as Miller rightly points out—is that students are not attracted to communication and media studies because these majors will make them "human" but rather because they will make them "money."

189

Miller recognizes well both what is gained by focusing attention on Humanities Two as well as what is lost. What is gained is a way to articulate the nature and value of the humanities to larger segments of the population. While undergraduate eyes may glaze over during philosophical lectures on democracy and citizenship, they perk up when the topic turns to television, film and video games—even if there is a philosophical subtext. What is often lost in pursuit of Humanities Two though is a sense of the larger context of communication and media. While students may become adept at new media production or video game design, without a concurrent understanding of their social, political, cultural, and economic dimensions, they risk becoming by vocation cogs in the wheels of creative industries that often run over people and despoil the environment.

Miller discusses this at length in a chapter entitled "Creative Industries—Credible Alternative?" It is an important chapter given the amount of national attention afforded the most visible advocate of the creative-industries approach, Richard Florida, who wrote the widely-cited book, *The Rise of the Creative Class and How It's Transforming Work, Leisure and Everyday Life* (2002). Florida's basic argument is that successful economic development can be had by supporting the growth of a technologically-savvy "creative class." This argument has made him a high-demand figure on the lecture circuit and an often-cited economic development authority. Miller points out that Florida even "trademarked" the phrase "creative class."

Miller's opening discussion of this topic is full of promise for the humanities. "Creative-industries discourse," writes Miller, "represents the most interesting and productive response/riposte to the crisis of the humanities I have seen." Not only does a creative-industries approach have "the potential to merge Humanities One and Two," it also holds promise for productive collaboration between the humanities and the sciences. In its idealized form, creative-industries might amount to "Humanities 2.0," that is, places where "[n]ew humanists apply technology to stories, and new scientists apply stories to technologies." Nevertheless, the creative industries response is not all sweetness and light.

"Today's discourse on the creative industries," comments Miller, "ignores such critical issues as the cognitariat, high-tech pollution, and cultural imperialism, not to mention the need to *understand* industries rather than celebrate them." For example, while digital technologies are often presented as ecologically friendly, the truth of the matter is that "[w]aste from discarded electronics is one of the biggest sources of heavy metals and toxic pollutants in the world's trash piles." And the list of horrors that follow from creative-industries practice goes on. Utilizing examples from the game industry, Miller traces the dark side of creative industries by revealing its connections to labor exploitation, military research, and the promotion of martial masculinity and youth violence. His conclusion is that the creative industries approach is deeply flawed with little or no potential to successfully merge Humanities One and Humanities Two.

So where does this humanities which is no longer one go from here? What alternative is there to "the banal Arnoldian training of Humanities One and the supine vocational training of Humanities Two and the creative industries"? Miller's response here is simple (and somewhat obvious given his Distinguished status in this area): the answer is "media and cultural studies." "The push for the study of media texts that reflect issues of consequence to the broad population," claims Miller, "can be central to renewing the humanities." A third way of looking at the humanities "must come from a blend of political economy, textual analysis, ethnography, and environmental studies such that students learn the materiality of how meaning is made, conveyed, and discarded." Rather than viewing the humanities as a group of disciplines, a cultural studies approach to renewing the humanities would encourage looking "across disciplines"—and promote the idea that "cultural studies" itself is not a discipline.

"Understanding culture requires studying it up, down, and sideways," writes Miller. This "means knowing which companies make texts, physical processes of production and distribution, systems of cross-subsidy and monopoly profit making, the complicity of educational canons with multinational corporations' business plans, and press coverage, inter alia." According to Miller, "a desirable cultural studies" is "a mixture of economics, politics, textual analysis, gender theory, ethnography, history, postcolonial theory, material objects, and policy, animated by a desire to reveal and transform those who control the means of communication and culture and undertaken with constant vigilance over one's raison d'être and modus operandi." Moreover, Miller's "desirable cultural studies" "takes its agenda and mode of analysis from economics, politics, media and communication studies, sociology, literature, education, the law, science and technology studies, environmentalism, anthropology, and history"—and he adds that its "focus is gender, race, class, and sexuality in everyday life, under the sign of a commitment to progressive social change." Miller's suggestions here raise a question: whether cultural studies is now trying to gain a second wind by trying to "repackage" itself as humanities. If so, this would be ironic because a few years earlier, the question was raised as to whether semiotics was trying to gain a second wind by trying to "repackage" itself as cultural studies. Repackaging ideas is this way is often regarded as an effective strategy of reselling older ideas to a newer audience.

The low road to meaning through the model of cultural studies advocated by Miller is not an easy one. There is no disciplinarity or interdisciplinary to lean on and there are no shortcuts to understanding. Nevertheless, Miller's suggestions for renewal in the humanities not only have the potential to re-energize the humanities, but also to offer a way out of the crisis in the humanities. The suggestion that the future of the humanities is held in the hands of cultural studies though is somewhat ironic—for discussions of the demise of cultural studies have been just as frequent as discussions of the demise of the humanities. As such, whether it is cultural studies that will be re-energizing the humanities *or* the humanities that will be re-energizing cultural studies is still to be determined. In any case, Miller's proposal has the capacity to re-energize both the humanities as well as cultural studies. Still, they require "blowing up" the two extant versions of the humanities: one that is described by Miller as "venerable and powerful and tends to determine how the sector is discussed in public"; and another that "is the humanities of state schools, which focus more on job prospects." How feasible is this? That is, how reasonable is it to expect respective proponents of Humanities One and Humanities Two to cede ground for the "new humanities," Humanities Three. Not very, I fear—and here's why.

For one, the birth of Humanities Three requires that the "venerable and powerful" Humanities One step aside or be cast aside as "King of the Humanities." And just how is this going to happen? Are the universities and endowed advocates of Humanities One like Nussbaum at the University of Chicago just going to step down?

Or does it mean that when they retire, they are replaced by "new humanists" like Miller? Also, how likely is it for an institution such as Harvard to close its philosophy department or Yale to shutter its English department in order to make way for the new cultural-studies-driven Humanities Three? Not very, for as Harvard English professor Louis Menand has noted in *The Marketplace of Ideas* (2010), "trying to reform the contemporary university is like trying to get on the Internet with a typewriter, or like trying to ride a horse to the mall."

Second, how do you wean students from "the other" humanities (Humanities Two) now that they can connect it with job prospects? Do the professors in these areas simply stop teaching "creative industries friendly" communication and media studies—and adopt instead Miller's "Humanities Three"? How likely is it that the state universities that employ them will allow them to offer this more progressive curriculum? Again, not very. Nevertheless—reform realities aside—there is a lot to be said in favor of Miller's approach to and proposal for resolving the crisis in the humanities.

Miller looks at the crisis in the humanities in a new and intriguing way. For him, the crisis is that today there are two humanities and neither is the right one. Moreover, rather than just describing the crisis and then walking away from it, Miller faces up to it with a proposal for reform and renewal in the humanities. And even though Humanities Three may only come to fruition in our distant future (as university reform *is* slow), Miller's proposal lends support to the notion that at least one aspect of renewal in the humanities can be institutionalized now. Namely, we can encourage proponents of both Humanities One and Humanities Two to take every opportunity that they can to help their students *understand how the university and the humanities work*; to encourage their students to examine the mutual and respective economics, politics, history, and policies of the university and the humanities; to ask how the university and the humanities produce, distribute, and dispose of knowledge; to learn how identities are formed within and by the university and the humanities; to help their students to imagine a world where both the university and the humanities work better—a world where the university is not always sovereign to the whims of the market, and the humanities are understood and valued. In the end, while Miller's proposals may not end the crisis in the humanities, discussions of their value inspired by his work may at least provide them with a reprieve.

193

24 | THE HUMANITIES TOOLBOX

The corporate university has not been kind to the humanities. Word on the street is that neoliberal educational practices and the growth of the corporate university are pushing the humanities toward demise.

But this is old news. Neoliberal academe is now normal academe. The notion that educational values are determined by market share is a commonplace one and the fact that majors and courses that cannot be directly connected to marketable skills and job attainment are at risk of extinction is well known. This situation puts advocates of the humanities in the dire position of either establishing strategies to slow down the decline and fall of the humanities at the hands of the corporate university or finding themselves gradually effaced and marginalized within the brave new world of higher education.

The Humanities and Public Life is a collective effort of some of the most celebrated and established figures in the humanities and related fields to fend off the destructive forces of the corporate university.[18] Called together by Peter Brooks, the Andrew W. Mellon Foundation Scholar at Princeton University, and the Sterling Professor Emeritus of Comparative Literature at Yale University, fifteen scholars, most of whom have named chairs or distinguished appointments, discuss some of the problems facing the humanities through a unique set-up.

Brooks says that after reading the "Torture Memos" released by the U.S. Department of Justice, where the use of torture was justified by "the most twisted, ingenious, perverse, and unethical interpretation of legal texts," he doubted such a justification could have been produced in good conscience by a person with a solid humanities education. "No one trained in the rigorous analysis of poetry," writes Brooks, "could possibly engage in such bad-faith interpretation without professional conscience intervening to say: this is not right." For Brooks, "the humanities can, and at their best do, represent a commitment to ethical reading."

Consequently, for Brooks, the notorious "Torture Memos" are more evidence of not only the continued need for "humanistic thought and analysis," as a humanist in good conscience would not have produced them, but also that the "close reading practiced in the humanities ought to be an export commodity to other fields, and it should take its place in public life." "The practice of reading itself, pursued with care and attention to language, its contexts, implications, uncertainties," comments the Andrew W. Mellon Foundation Scholar, "can itself be an ethical act."

To explore these claims and related ones, Brooks organized a symposium called "The Humanities in the Public Sphere." The material in this book is the product of this symposium. It includes a keynote lecture by Judith Butler, followed by essays from Elaine Scarry, Charles Larmore, Patricia J. Williams, Ralph J. Hexter, Jonathan Lear, and Paul W. Kahn. The essays are then grouped into twos, and receive responses by two or three additional scholars. The respondents are Kwame Anthony Appiah, Jonathan Culler, Derek Attridge, Richard Sennett, Michael Roth, William Germano, Kim Lane Scheppele, and Didier Fassin. Finally, after each of the three sub-groups of essays and responses, there is a brief discussion that includes all of the participants as well as some audience members. The volume concludes with a discussion among all of the participants.

Butler's keynote, "Ordinary, Incredulous," is a beautiful defense of critique, in Fassin's words, "as thinking against the obvious." She finds it "quite incredulous" that the neoliberal world now makes it necessary for us to defend the public value of a basic humanities education. For her, the ability to "learn to think, to work with language and images, and to read, to make sense, to intervene, to take apart, to formulate evaluative judgments and even to make the world anew" is "obvious" and that we now need to be able to defend them is "quite incredulous." But such is the central task of the humanities in the age of neoliberalism—one that is made even more difficult when combined with "anti-intellectual conservativism."

While aware of the most common arguments in defense of the humanities, Butler is critical of most of them. These include "the humanities have intrinsic value; the humanities are useless, and that is their value; public intellectuals exemplify the value of the humanities for public life; the humanities offer certain kinds of skill development that are important for economic mobility; [and] the humanities offer certain kinds of literacy that are indispensable to citizenship." However, she has an affinity for one of the common lines of defense of the humanities, namely, "the humanities offer a critical perspective on values that can actively engage the contemporary metrics of value by which the humanities are weakened, if not destroyed." In other words, the value of the humanities is to be found in its measure of measure.

"Oddly," writes Butler,

> our very capacity for critically re-evaluating is what cannot be measured by the metrics by which the humanities are increasingly judged. This means the resource we need to save the humanities is precisely one that has been abandoned by the metrics that promise to save the humanities if only we comply. So perhaps we must retrieve from the threat of oblivion those ways of valuing that can put into perspective the closing of the horizons enacted by the metrics we are asked to use. These are metrics of forgetfulness, perhaps, or metrics of effacement, conduits to oblivion, where the calculus emerges as the final arbiter of value, which means that the values we have to defend are already lost. This does not mean that we become conservative, endeavoring to reinstate a former time; rather, we must move forward in new ways, through new idioms, and with some impurity, to reanimate the very ideals that guide and justify our work.

Butler is less asking us to save the humanities than to protect the path that allows us to "move forward in new ways, through new idioms." And "if obscurity is sometimes the necessary corrective to what has become obvious, so be it." Her argument in defense of obscurity as a corrective to the obvious, the ordinary, is also one against the transparency of neoliberalism. "This means," concludes Butler, "that we exercise critical judgment in the breach, reentering the obscure into the obvious in order to affirm what is left between us still to lose, to keep, to keep animated."

197

Fittingly enough this point is also the final comment in the volume. The metrics used by neoliberal academe need to themselves be evaluated, "we need ways of evaluating our own work that rival or contest some of the notions of assessment." "I think we need to reanimate critique," says Butler, "as precisely a way of thinking about the competing schemes of evaluation and evaluating them."

Butler's keynote is a powerful one and in many ways dominates the volume, particularly her claim in the final line of the book: "We have to figure out a measure for measure." As a call for critique in face of the neoliberal politics that justifies the very "Torture Memos" that motivated Brooks to organize the symposium, Butler in a way short circuits the power of many of the excellent engagements regarding the ethics of reading. As the volume demonstrates, she is a tough act to follow.

Though beautifully argued and written, the essays and responses in Part One, "Is There an Ethics of Reading?," feel dated after Butler's keynote, particularly Charles Larmore's essay, "The Ethics of Reading," with its invocation of J. Hillis Miller circa 1989 and E. D. Hirsch on validity in interpretation circa 1965. Though Larmore cannot be faulted for addressing a topic set by Brooks, his engagement reminds us that the ethics of reading was more of an issue in the age of deconstruction than it is in the age of new media—and even old media like television and film. Scarry on the ethical power of literature, particularly the way in which it contributes to the diminution of injury through beauty is itself beautiful, though as an argument in defense of the humanities against the neoliberal onslaught, it is not as persuasive as Butler's measure of measure.

Part Two, "The Ethics of Reading and the Professions," continues to explore Brooks's claim that the "commitment, and the training and discipline of close reading that underlies it, represents something that we as teachers of the humanities need to bring to other fields, especially those that undertake the training of professional readers such as lawyers, whose work includes interpretation." Patricia Williams discusses "how things live in language and how we objectify in a way that is eventually translated in and into law." Her analysis of three captions to photos taken in the wake of the Haiti earthquake reveals the ways in which naming plays a role in the ethics of reading, particularly in the eyes of the law. However, the highlight of the essay is her description of how a woman sharing a bench with her at an airport came to engage her in a conversation about the aftermath of the Haiti earthquake—a conversation she resisted until she became aware that the woman on the bench had first-hand knowledge of the aftermath.

The second essay in Part Two is from classicist and University of California, Davis, provost Ralph Hexter, who uses the occasion to discuss challenges faced by university leaders who desire to read ethically. His discussion of "corporate reading," which he describes as a "shared interpretive labor" wherein our individual "ethical awareness" can "slip between the cracks, get lost in the shuffle, or simply be eclipsed by the immensity of the process itself," is one of the most intriguing ones in the book.

Hexter's essay reveals some key problems of managerial reading in the neoliberal university, specifically, ones where the structures of the university provide fertile conditions for unethical reading such as those demonstrated in the "Torture Memos." It is at this point that the "ethics" of reading in neoliberal academe clearly became more a discussion of the "politics" of reading, that is, a discussion not of how individuals read texts, but rather of how groups within the university become complicit in unethical reading through shared interpretive labor.

The strongest and most interesting response in the volume is also contained in this section. And it is also by a university administrator, Wesleyan president, Michael Roth, who in three pages undermines much of the project of the symposium. First, in opposition to Hexter, he says that he does "not believe there are noninstrumental administrative ways of reading." Roth continues:

> I always look for my wallet whenever I hear about noninstrumental administrative anything, because bureaucratic instrumentality can never be noninstrumental. I think the bureaucratization of the university, of which I am a part, is a horrible feature of university life. I can sleep at night (sometimes) because I think, being part of that bureaucratic instrumentality, I preserve the possibility for my colleagues to do the wonderful work that people are doing in conferences like this.

199

The rubber of this symposium hits the road of neoliberal academe in this comment by Roth. If he is right, and there is no way to provide a measure for the humanities within the university that is not instrumental, then we are doomed to increasing bureaucratization of the university and its deepening neoliberalization. Fortunately,

Roth's opinion is the minority opinion in this volume, but it reveals a taste of the opposition facing the humanities within the neoliberal university.

However, Roth makes another point that is equally as controversial. He asks about "what to do with the potential ethical value of other imaginative activities" such as watching television? Is watching television "more or less ethical than reading"? Roth's question goes to one raised earlier as to whether the question asked by Brooks is more in line with the age of the print or the age of new media? That is, the age of reading or the age of viewing? Though it does not get very much discussion in this volume, the question of whether the ethics of reading is the best way to describe the outcome of a solid humanities education in the new millennium versus say the ethics of watching, listening, or texting is a good one. What, for example, is the relationship between "close reading" and "close viewing"? For that matter, how do we square the movement today toward "surface reading" in the humanities with calls such as the one in this volume for a return to "close reading"? For the most part, the essays in this volume leave these questions unanswered.

In the final part of the book, Part Three, the question of the ethics of reading is extended from the professional context of law and university administration to the world of human rights within the context of the humanities. Jonathan Lear's essay on how he came to be interested in Crow history and culture is one of the highlights of the volume. It is centered around his changing understanding of a quote attributed to Chief Plenty Coups, the "last great chief of the Crow tribe," who said the following about life after the move to the reservation: "After the buffalo went, the hearts of my people fell to the ground and we could not lift them up again. After this, nothing happened."

Lear explains that when he began to work on the Crow, he thought that they "had faced a catastrophic trauma and were now living in its historical aftermath." Now he thinks "the trauma persists in the present." His conclusion is that the humanities are important to us now more than ever. Not because of their advocacy for the plight of others. Rather, because they awaken us. "We need the poetic words of another," comments Lear, "to *wake us up.*" Though it is not easy for him to say "what this consists of," it is still nonetheless a strong argument in favor of the humanities amidst the somatic forces of the neoliberal university.

Lear's essay also gives us a good perspective on the troubles facing the humanities in particular, and the university in general. Too many read the words "the humanities are in peril" but never awaken from their neoliberal slumbers. The humanities are asleep within the world of the corporate university and Lear is challenging us to awaken them. In much the same spirit of Butler who argues that the critical powers of the humanities are what is needed to assess the assessment that is killing them, so too is Lear arguing that we need to look toward the poetic words of others to wake us up to the central value of the humanities, namely its ability to help us understand the sad condition of the present. How trauma persists; how racism persists; how inequality persists. The list goes on.

The essay by Lear is a powerful defense of the humanities because it demonstrates the value of the humanities through its practice. But Roth's response too is powerful because it shows the formidable opposition of instrumental bureaucracy situated amidst the enabling context of neoliberalism. Moreover, to be fair to all of the other contributors, there is much to be liked in their work too, which is no surprise given that this is a collection from many of academe's luminaries.

Butler is right that we should "avoid seeing the humanities as a set of tools that can be applied." In a way, though, her contributions go in the opposite direction of the one established by Brooks, that is, to find in "close reading" "an export commodity to other fields." For how different is viewing close reading as a commodity from viewing it as a tool to be applied in other professions? The essays in this volume present a great case study of how the instrumental thinking of the corporate university keeps pulling us back to viewing the humanities as a tool set that can be used in vocational or professional training. Lear though bursts this bubble by getting us to think outside of the ordinary in the humanities, that is, cold "studies" and often empty "advocacy" scholarship. He points to a way for "something to happen again" in the humanities on the reservation of higher education. And, after all, isn't this what we in the humanities are really after? Namely, a reawakening of the humanities amidst calls for their demise from neoliberal academe? One wonders though if this is even possible

201

now that the humanities are widely regarded as nothing more than a toolbox used to improve vocational and professional training.

Selling the humanities has to be more than just selling tools—for if not, it makes us into nothing more than clerks at a hardware store for neoliberalism.

AFTERWORD

PRACTICING THE FRAGMENT
by H. Aram Veeser

"You've got to push the limits."

—Jeffrey R. Di Leo, "Tumbling Dice" (2020)

Selling the Humanities is a book that investigates the ways in which the humanities are valued. The most egregious of these ways is the demand to know—"right now, dammit!"—the actual cash worth of the humanities in exact dollar figures. Such calls for a strict accounting come from college administrators, state legislatures, journalists, parents of every race and class, and above all students themselves. All are asking, how much should we be expected to pay for this stuff? What is the return on investment? The book leads with an epigraph from philosopher Judith Butler: *If the humanities are to make a difference in public life, does that mean we have to say that they are instrumental to some other social good?* Author Di Leo translates her question more bluntly: the humanities are thought to have value only as a step-stool to more lucrative callings—a ladder to be kicked away as quickly as possible.

As a long-time university dean himself and a publisher, author Jeffrey Di Leo knows the cash nexus. He is a prominent figure who founded a well-known scholarly journal that has been growing for 30 years, who edits a book series and a bi-monthly book review, the director of the Society for Critical Exchange, and the author or editor of thirty-five books. He understands business. Many of these chapters are filled with figures, percentages, facts, and trends. His statistics prove that the economic crisis of 2008 has turned the humanities into a moneymaking scheme, with badly paid, unorganized labor hauling 70% of the teaching load and student loans outpacing credit card debt. Philosophically, he is a materialist not an idealist. He comes down hard on bloviating academics and pundits and even chides famously hard-headed public intellectual Stanley Fish, who, while pricking humanists' self-importance and assuring them that professing literature was "just a job," seemed to forget this humility when he told governors, trustees, and wealthy citizens to mind their own business and leave the humanities to the academics. Di Leo gives a refreshingly hard-left turn to Fish's position and argues that "it was academics who did not know the principles of management and marketing." He brings gallows humor to his account of Pharrell Williams's hit record, "Be Happy," a song whose history and sales figures prove Di Leo's point that everything is for sale, including happiness. He deflates well-insulated elites who protest the way of the world. When the revered philosopher and public intellectual Martha Nussbaum grimly intones, for example, "The future of democracies hangs in the balance," he punctures her inflationary account of the world-transforming "skills" learned in humanities classes. He regrets that History and Literature and Philosophy are subsiding into helpmeet or sidekick status—maybe they won't even be academic departments after a while. But their demotion is also a kind of arrival, signaling their new *it-goes-without-saying* status. Proclaiming the humanities to be central is not only implausible. It is also square. Secondariness may well be preferable. Footholds on the margin become dangerous supplements in his own theoretical tradition. The edges are charged up with dynamic potentiality.

Selling the Humanities (note the touch of crass in the title) surveys the various ways in which the humanities are being marketed, sold, and turned to a profit. The book is a high-speed tour comprising twenty-four brief (3000 word) essays. You move past these exhibits not shuffling along behind a lugubrious museum docent but rather speeding in a red El Dorado convertible. Di Leo barrels through the essential topics: music, self-publishing, illustrated pocketbooks, abandoned libraries, popular writers, a few thinker-celebrities like Harold Bloom (chapters 13 and 18) and Bertrand Russell. The ride has some veering leans and hairpin turns. After all, there's an intellectual Thelma and Louise at the wheel. Or is he the Stones' Keith Richards, writing songs using the Bill Burroughs cut-up method: ripping headlines out of newspapers and throwing them on the floor and seeing what comes up. Di Leo self-knowingly calls his method a pulverized discourse or a practice of the fragment. Yet, although he favorably cites Gide's assertion that incoherence is preferable to a distorting order, the book is distinguished by inspiration and drive.

Chapter 1 takes up happiness journalism, "Happy" by Keith Richards at Nellcôte, a song that was written one night in 1971, "it just came tripping off the tongue," while "Happy" by Pharrell Williams's "Happy," from 2007 in the neoliberal era (N.E.), went through 11 rejections and revisions. Later chapters examine the B.N.E. aura of old-school personal journals of Gide, Barthes, and Sontag, with Di Leo explaining why a handwritten diary or journal beats emails any day, or why vinyl records beat digital, tape, MP3 formats, and why books and "book buildings" beat JSTOR and Gutenberg.com, and overall why vintage materiality beats high tech abstractions. A more disturbing example comes in a chapter called "Wax Power" about technologies of sound. Here, Adolf Hitler is quoted from the *Manual of German Radio* published in 1938: "Without the loudspeaker, we would never have conquered Germany." Hitler seems to have given loudspeakers a dose of Svengali-style aura, while corporate giant Amazon is as repulsive as the dung-beetle protagonist of Kafka's *Metamorphosis*. Amazon in publishing is like a gigantic insect on one's dinner plate. Di Leo's refreshing take on the age of mechanical reproduction also includes music. Chapter 16, "Music Contra Life," offers a sophisticated reading of Nietzsche's revulsion by the music of Richard Wagner as music fit only for a sick people (the German people). Di Leo connects Nietzsche's "sickness" to Foucault's biopower. Riveting detours include chapters on "desk rejection" as a way to pre-empt peer review of hot-potato journal submissions and on Amy Hungerford's post-humanist theories, for example, the idea that delivery trucks are also contributing authors to certain works of literature. Another great chapter recounts an atrocious episode: City College of New York hired philosopher Bertrand Russell in 1941, only to have moralistic citizens, political demagogues, and journalists start a campaign to rescind the offer. CCNY resisted, and so the governor of New York State simply cut the free-thinking Russell's tenured line. The story comes back to the fragile state of the humanities. We have today elitist pontificators squaring off against philistines who say universities should train people exclusively for jobs. Di Leo explores various "third ways" promising a way out of this sterile dichotomy, for example, Richard Florida's call to encourage the growth of a technologically-savvy "creative class." But such repackagings are countered by Louis Menand, who

205

contends that reforming the humanities is like trying to get onto the internet with a typewriter. And so the impasse remains intact. In his final chapter, "The Humanities Toolbox," Di Leo endorses another of Judith Butler's claims, to the effect that the humanities' "capacity for critically re-evaluating is what cannot be measured by the metrics by which the humanities are increasingly judged." He agrees that humanities are the measure of all tool-ness, and he also finds in the humanities' "close reading" "an export commodity to other fields." This is where *Selling the Humanities* comes to an end. Is this the final destination, or a rest stop?

The looming problem is that the humanities, stuck in their creaky technological past, have no fungible value. Vinyl records, decaying books, abandoned libraries, the humanities: Di Leo sees opportunity in things that have lost their customer base.

Titling one's book *Selling the Humanities* leads of course to the question, So Who is Buying? Who in the neoliberal marketplace is ready to pay good money to write term papers on Provençal poetry or the battle plans of Lao Tzu? Who whips out a checkbook to fund vague wispy notions like critical thinking, empathy, democratic values, and cultural awareness? Would these airy boomer nostrums convince the Tik Tok generation? Di Leo states bluntly what every professor knows: "*Few things are more painful for faculty than trying to convince students that their time and money is not being wasted through the study of topics they regard as superfluous.*"

Pain levels go up to a seven or eight when Di Leo audits the publishing trade. When he reveals that no one needs credentials to publish a "learned" book—or ten books—we want to call for our painkiller. Self-published books, formerly "vanity press" embarrassments, today outnumber peer-vetted books by three-to-one. Di Leo defends self-publishing—intellectual ferment, anti-corporate rebellion—but many people would immediately think of Gresham's Law: bad money drives out good. Thousands upon thousands of books go unnoticed and unread, the chaff smothering the wheat. Di Leo describes the Espresso Book Machine, a vending unit that spits out books, plainly a Swiftian contraption, like extracting sunbeams from cucumbers or reducing excrement to its original food. *Gulliveresque* too are the many respectable publishing houses that have branched out to offer package deals for self-publishing your book under their respectable imprimatur; and ghostwriters have always been around but now they openly promise to write your new book from scratch. We have self-driving cars, and we soon will have DIY computer publishing software. After describing these cash cows, Di Leo concludes mildly, poker-face intact, that *self-publishing is the major book production force in the United States.*

Artisanal stuff like writing books and conducting seminars are exiting stage right, while media and communications settle in comfortably amidst the ruins. The mere antiquity of humanities fields won't save them, any more than it saved New York or Chicago from devastating urban renewals to build interstate highways through them. The 140-year-old liberal arts await the wrecking ball, just as the 2,500-year-old olive orchards fell before the bulldozer. STEM is siphoning off the artesian springs of money. English and History are sluicing down to Hades where they will join Classics and Philosophy, expecting a dim afterlife as odd hobbies for eccentric idlers with independent incomes. Can anything prevent the humanities from turning into *a non-essential, educational "luxury" item*? Di Leo wants the humanities to take back the land they lost to filmmaking, web-management, digital design, the higher Tweeting. But he knows better than to say if any will work. No one can say. The humanities are in raggedy flight.

A book entitled, like this one, *Selling the Humanities* has to believe that buyers may be found. Shipping the humanities into adjacent fields is as close as Di Leo comes to a strategic recommendation. Di Leo dares to imagine at least a limited return to the balance of trade that defined High Theory: *exporting them* [the humanities] *to the professional sides and ends of the academic house.* Would this mean humanities professors explaining to MCA and film departments how to handle not just Jane Austen novels but also deconstruction, queer theory, and Afrofuturism? Fat chance.

Di Leo grounds his limited optimism in the data. While study of the humanities has declined since the 1970s, business enrollments have picked up (rising 176%) and communication and media studies (rising 616%) are off the charts. The business of education is booming. His enterprising, mergers-and-acquisitions temperament inclines him to see opportunities. He finds hope, for example, in signs that a major "repackaging" is underway. Perhaps cultural studies is trying to make itself over as humanities, just as a few years earlier semiotics tried to repackage itself as cultural studies. "Newer" disciplines (actually quite old now) now called various "Studies," such as Black, LGBTQ, Disability, and Latinx, are often institutionally homeless. To them, the old humanities departments must look like those abandoned steel mills on

the banks of the Monongahela. Cultural studies and MFA programs eye these vacating institutional spaces as a standing temptation. Semiotics and cultural studies are like the cuckoo, searching for ways to lay eggs in someone else's nest.

The elephant in the room is MFA programs. Why are writing programs thriving whilst traditional literature programs are tanking? Like communication and media studies with their snowballing enrollments, creative writing programs are busting out at the seams. Where does neoliberalism find the business logic to mass producing MFAs? Di Leo is too canny to offer facile solutions to these puzzling facts.

Academic book sales are going fairly strong. He reports that while the overall number of exhibitors at the MLA has dropped (by 35 percent), the number of university presses exhibiting at the MLA has actually risen (by 37 percent). Better yet, all of the university presses who exhibited at the 1969 MLA are still publishing scholarly books 50 years later. Amazingly, we still have goods for export.

Di Leo has good things to say about books published by non-university presses as well. He praises illustrated introductions to philosophy and theory and history, for-beginners handbooks, and popularizing digests. This sort of work is scorned by "real" scholars, but Di Leo nobly rises above such carping. Specialists are perfectly right to be alarmed, he says, because now these complacent specialists will have to learn to write as interestingly as H. G. Wells or Allison Bechdel or Lin-Manuel Miranda.

On the style tip, Di Leo's wildest and most brilliant interventions always involve music. He grounds his aesthetic on Nietzsche ("Without music, life would be an error") updated by Keith Richards ("If you don't make bold moves, you don't get fucking anywhere"). He responds to Rita Felski's attacks on the hermeneutics of suspicion by appealing to Elvis Presley's last chart topping single, "Suspicious Minds." Felski has turned against the kind of criticism that unmasks, exposes, or delates political evils that are discoverable inside a superficially anodyne text. Di Leo citing Elvis proclaims suspicion a good gig, *We're caught in a trap/We can't get out/ We should go on together in the humanities with suspicious minds.* He is unmoved by Frankfurt school hand-wringing, by Adornian complaints that music deceitfully solves real-world problems with soothing fantasies. Instead, he promotes music as a tangible good that disrupts the strict cash nexus of neoliberalism. He backs up his aestheticism by siding with Nietzsche's view: *aesthetics is nothing but a kind of applied physiology.* Di Leo feels that a biopolitics of music like the amplifiers of Hitler can override economics and all humanity itself. Just as Nietzsche wrote that the music of Richard Wagner was unhealthy and had made people in Germany sick, Di Leo feels that the Rolling Stones et al. conversely can impart a certain kind of health and energy, in fact a refreshing the will to live.

Jeffrey Di Leo is above all else a professional philosopher. He quotes Plato's "Apology of Socrates" in order to prove that apologies are philosophically potent—and more pointedly to excoriate the neo-liberal non-apologies often made by #MeToo offenders: "I am so sorry you feel that I offended you." Such apologies lack all regret and invalidate the speech act of apologizing. Not only apologies a la Socrates but also philosophical pessimism taken from Schopenhauer underpin Di Leo's thinking. Nietzsche's love for music and his respect for music's power are very much a part of Di Leo's intellectual formation. If Wagner can be enjoyed only by the sickest Germans, as Nietzsche says, then Di Leo takes this further, using Foucault to ask, Which musicians make music sick, which writers today make writing sick? Beyond Plato, Schopenhauer, Nietzsche, and Foucault, Di Leo makes intriguing use of object-oriented ontology. iPhones can be actors, and delivery trucks, and celebrity: all are purposive yet non-human. By mobilizing outré, off-beat, even bankrupt categories, like the vinyl record and the rotting book, Di Leo performs a radical intervention that could be nicknamed object-oriented aesthetics. Aesthetic objects would no longer be valued for their metaphysical links to deathless ideas or for their expression of admired political positions, but rather they would be prized for their linguistic instability and capacity to be interpreted in many different ways. Di Leo's example of such instability is famous critic Harold Bloom proclaiming Philip Roth's permanent place as a comic genius; and simultaneously the equally categorical rejection of Roth's comic misogyny by a #MeToo conference panel. The example begins to suggest the outline of Di Leo's impressive effort to articulate what he calls a *negative dialogics.*

This book confronts a nasty crisis with a level head. Distinguished by a light touch and independence of thought, the author brings a steady eye to the often-preposterous idealist claims made for the humanities. He addresses many more topics and issues than I have been able to discuss. The wide range of his experience as dean, publisher, editor, and author well suits his Wildean sense that criticism is the strongest autobiography. The book reads like a high-speed, cross-country auto race with pit stops at key cultural sites, a "practice of the fragment" that boasts a noble philosophical lineage stretching from Gide and Gramsci to Barthes and Wayne Koestenbaum. After reams of self-involved ritual ululation over the decline of the humanities, the riffs of a worldly critic are deeply welcome. In a distressing moment on the south Texas coast, where neoliberalism is practically a left-wing stance, Di Leo finds succor, understandably, in tales of the Rolling Stones, stuck in a decaying mansion near Monte Carlo, fighting the damp while composing great songs. Like them he has rolled the dice and to some degree has beaten the odds. This book in particular includes liberal doses of the Devil's Chord, cheering on the advent of self-publishing, recommending a wholesale revision of the humanities, celebrating suspicion and indeed calling for more. Like a great vinyl LP, *Selling the Humanities* makes a coherent statement from cuts that can each stand on their own.

ACKNOWLEDGMENTS

I am indebted to the *American Book Review* and its Reading Series for affording me the opportunity to be in the company of some of the most gifted writers and inspiring critics in America.

This would not have been possible without tremendous community support from Victoria, Texas, which became—in the words of *Inside Higher Ed*—"an unlikely haven for humanities publishing."

It would also not have taken place without the guidance and encouragement of many individuals, especially R. M. Berry and the late Charles Harris. In 2005, these two remarkable individuals set me on a journey to the peripheries of the humanities where writerly writing and small-press publishing flourish, a place that is now my intellectual home as I continue to serve as editor-in-chief of *American Book Review*.

Most of the essays in this volume first appeared in the *American Book Review* from 2017 to 2020. However, Chapters 17, 21, 22, and 24 were previously published in *The Comparatist*, and Chapters 13, 18, and 23 in *symplokē*. All are used here with permission.

These essays have benefitted from the insightful conversations and timely suggestions of many individuals including Frederick Luis Aldama, Charles Alexander, Mark Amerika, Charles Bernstein, Jake Blevins, Amaranth Borsuk, Stephen J. Burn, Robert Coover, Kwame Dawes, Debra Di Blasi, Rikki Ducornet, Brian Evenson, Nick Flynn, Ru Freeman, Robin Truth Goodman, Peter Hitchcock, Nalo Hopkinson, Christine Hume, Shelley Jackson, Charles Johnson, Stephen Graham Jones, A. Van Jordan, Michael Joyce, Amitava Kumar, Sophia A. McClennen, Anthony Madrid, Ben Marcus, Carole Maso, Cris Mazza, E. Ethelbert Miller, Paul Allen Miller, Paul D. Miller aka DJ Spooky, Christian Moraru, Warren Motte, John Mowitt, Duane Niatum, the late John O'Brien, Daniel T. O'Hara, Brian O'Keeffe, Marjorie Perloff, Jean-Michel Rabaté, Saba Razvi, Jeffrey A. Sartain, Kyle Schlesinger, Nicole Simek, Henry Sussman, Joseph Tabbi, Steve Tomasula, John Tytell, H. Aram Veeser, and Zahi Zalloua.

A special note of appreciation goes out to Keri Ruiz and J. J. Hernandez for their editorial support; to Vikki Fitzpatrick and Paula Edging for administrative support; to H. Aram Veeser for penning the afterword to this book; to J. Bruce Fuller for his help in steering this manuscript through the publication process; and to the many individuals that have generously supported the American Book Review Endowment.

Finally, I would like to thank my wife Nina for her unfailing encouragement, support, and patience.

NOTES

1   The sixteen countries from the 1951 report are Union of South Africa, Dominican Republic, Nicaragua, Panama, United States, Argentina, Ceylon, Lebanon, Philippines, Austria, Belgium, Bulgaria, Denmark, Finland, France, and Germany.

2   January 2019.

3   January 2019.

4   Harold Bloom, *Possessed by Memory: The Inward Light of Criticism* (New York: Alfred A. Knopf, 2019).

5   Bloom submitted this reply on June 15, 2019—and would pass away four months later, on October 14, 2019.

6   November 27, 2018.

7   September 2018.

8   Amy Hungerford, *Making Literature Now* (Stanford: Stanford University Press, 2016).

9   Harold Bloom, *The American Canon: Literary Genius from Emerson to Pynchon*, ed. David Mikics (New York: Library of America, 2019).

10 Bloom completed for publication *Take Arms Against a Sea of Troubles: The Power of the Reader's Mind Over a Universe of Death* (2020) and *The Bright Book of Life: Novels to Read and Reread* (2020) before his death in 2019. Given his prolixity, one assumes as well that other book manuscripts will appear posthumously.

11 September 2018.

12 October 2018.

13 October 11, 2018.

14 2017.

15 Kathleen Fitzpatrick, *Generous Thinking: A Radical Approach to Saving the University* (Baltimore, MD: Johns Hopkins University Press, 2019).

16 Martha C. Nussbaum, *Not for Profit: Why Democracy Needs the Humanities* (Princeton and Oxford: Princeton University Press, 2010).

17 Toby Miller, *Blow Up the Humanities* (Philadelphia, PA: Temple University Press, 2012).

18 Peter Brooks, ed. with Hilary Jewett, *The Humanities and Public Life* (New York: Fordham University Press, 2014).

SOURCES

1. "Happiness for Sale." *American Book Review* 41.6 (September/October 2020).

2. "The Writer's Journal." *American Book Review* 41.5 (July/August 2020).

3. "Industrial Disease." *American Book Review* 41.3 (March/April 2020).

4. "The Speed of Publishing." *American Book Review* 41.4 (May/June 2020).

5. "Suspicious Minds." *American Book Review* 41.2 (January/February 2020).

6. "The Town Book Building." *American Book Review* 41.1 (November/December 2019).

7. "Dark Shadows." *American Book Review* 40.6 (September/October 2019).

8. "The Self-Publishing Revolution." *American Book Review* 40.5 (July/August 2019).

9. "Tumbleweed Connections." *American Book Review* 40.4 (May/June 2019).

10. "Wax Power." *American Book Review* 40.3 (March/April 2019).

11. "A Fig Leaf for Literature." *American Book Review* 40.2 (January/February 2019).

12. "Fashionable Philosophy." *American Book Review* 40.1 (November/December 2018).

13. "Dead Criticism." Review of Harold Bloom's *Possessed by Memory: The Inner Light of Criticism*, with A Reply from Harold Bloom. *symplokē* 27.1/2 (2019).

14. "Don't Shoot the Journal Editor." *American Book Review* 39.5 (July/August 2018).

15. "Does Philosophy Need a Story?" *American Book Review* 39.4 (May/June 2018).

16. "Music contra Life." *American Book Review* 39.2/3 (January-April 2018).

17. Review of Amy Hungerford's *Making Literature Now*. *The Comparatist* 42 (2018).

18. "American Literature in Bloom." Review of Harold Bloom's *The American Canon: Literary Genius from Emerson to Pynchon*. *symplokē* 28.1/2 (2020).

19. "Philosophy without Apologies." *American Book Review* 39.6 (September/October 2018).

20. "Freethinkers, Heretics, and the Little Blue Books." *American Book Review* 39.1 (November/December 2017).

21. Review of Kathleen Fitzpatrick's *Generous Thinking: A Radical Approach to Saving the University*. *The Comparatist* 44 (2020).

22. Review of Martha Nussbaum's *Not for Profit: Why Democracy Needs the Humanities*. *The Comparatist* 37 (2013).

23. "This Humanities Which Is Not One." *symplokē* 20.1/2 (2012).

24. Review of Peter Brooks, ed., *The Humanities and Public Life*. *The Comparatist* 40 (2016).